W9-CQT-988

Surfing Illustrated

AN ILLUSTRATED GUIDE TO WAVE RIDING

WRITTEN AND ILLUSTRATED
BY
JOHN ROBISON

INTERNATIONAL MARINE / McGRAW-HILL EDUCATION
CAMDEN, MAINE • NEW YORK • CHICAGO • SAN FRANCISCO • ATHENS • LONDON •
MADRID • MEXICO CITY • MILAN • NEW DELHI • SINGAPORE • SYDNEY • TORONTO

DEDICATED TO MY MOM,
WHO ENCOURAGED ME TO
GO FOR THE BIG WAVES.

5 6 7 8 9 10 DOC/DOC 1 0 9 8 7 6 5 4

ISBN 978-0-07-147742-0
MHID 0-07-147742-X
eBook 0-07-174814-8

Library of Congress Cataloging-in-Publication Data

Robison, John, 1966–
     Surfing illustrated : an illustrated guide to wave riding /
written and illustrated by John Robison.
          176 p. : ill. ; 23 cm.
     ISBN 0-07-147742-X
     Includes index.
          1. Surfing — Handbooks, manuals, etc.
GV840.SB R63 2010
797.3'2

                                        2010017223

Questions regarding the content of this book should be
addressed to www.internationalmarine.com

Questions regarding the ordering of this book should be
addressed to
McGraw-Hill Education
Customer Service Department
P.O. Box 547
Blacklick, OH 43004
Retail customers: 1-800-262-4729
Bookstores: 1-800-722-4726

Printed on 50 Environ Print.
Illustrations by John Robison.
Design by John Barnett / 4 Eyes Design.

WARNING

Surfing is an inherently hazardous sport and carries risks of
serious injury, trauma, and drowning. This book is not intended
to replace instruction by a qualified instructor or to substitute
for good judgment. In using this book, the reader releases the
author, publisher, and distributor from liability for any injury,
including death, that might result. It is understood that you surf
at your own risk.

CONTENTS

ACKNOWLEDGMENTS

Writing a book is a lot like learning to surf. The vast majority of the time you are flailing with no end in sight. You rely on your friends for advice and encouragement. But when you catch a wave and stand up, or see that your work helped someone else stand up, you realize it is all worth it.

I would like to thank the folks who helped make this book a reality. First, I'd like to thank Ed Guzman with Club Ed Surf School in Santa Cruz, California. Ed has spent his career teaching people how to surf and offered his sage advice throughout the writing of this book. I highly recommend his surf lessons and surf camps to anyone who wants to learn from the best (see Club-Ed.com). Rocky Snyder, author of *Fit to Surf,* also pointed me in the right direction to start the research for this book. Cary Smith, Deputy Harbormaster with Pillar Point Harbor, Half Moon Bay, California, contributed to the section on surf rescues. My longtime surfing buddies Joe Archibald, Sean Baker, and Julian Meisler all offered excellent suggestions based on their years of experience.

Tony and Lib Johnson of Mr. Surfs Surf Shop, in Panama City Beach, Florida, showed some real aloha spirit and gave me some great standup paddleboard tips. And thanks to the good folks at YOLO boards (yoloboard.com) for letting me try their newest standup paddleboards.

Special thanks to Bob Penuelas, the cartoonist of the terrific Wilbur Kookmeyer series (wilbur-kookmeyer.com), for being a longtime inspiration to me.

Thanks yet again to Bob Holtzman, Jon Eaton, and Molly Mulhern with International Marine/ McGraw-Hill for all their help and patience in transforming my surf scribbles into this book. Fellow inland surfer Marcy Westover provided some good yoga tips.

My wife Angel has earned a big smooch and a squeeze for putting up with me throughout this process. Now we can continue with our mini-adventures!

PREFACE

The word "stoked" is a surfing term used to describe "a profound state of enthusiasm" for something, usually a wave or a surf session or something else exciting. As my friends can attest, I am extremely enthusiastic about surfing. Like so many high school students, I was reprimanded regularly for doodling cartoons of epic tube rides in class. Despite my awe-inspiring, imaginary maneuvers, I did not grow up to be a professional surfer. I am just one of countless intermediate surfers who are incredibly stoked every time they get in the water and go surfing.

My goal is to share my sense of stoke with other folks out there. Yes, the waves can be crowded and this book may make the waves even more crowded. But my hope is that readers will use the tips in this book to be safer in the water, to use proper etiquette to better share the waves, and to take better care of our coastal environment.

The environmental problems suffered by our oceans and coastlines are not as bad as they appear. They are worse. We will not take better care of these special places until we have a personal stake in restoring them. I am donating a portion of the royalties to conservation groups like the Surfrider Foundation and encourage anyone who appreciates the magic of water to support their excellent work.

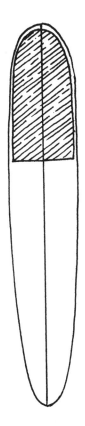

INTRODUCTION

If you've ever had the inkling that you wanted to try surfing, then consider this book as your official invitation to get started.

Although surfing may look like a lot of fun, until you try it you have no concept of how amazingly fun it really is. Catching a wave is simply one of the best sensations in life. I'm talking about ear-to-ear grins and an inability to paddle back to shore without "just one more wave." The classic slang surfer word "stoked" is often used to describe this emotion.

After that sales pitch, I would be remiss if I did not also tell you that surfing is one of the hardest sports to learn. To accomplish some state of proficiency, you will need to spend several weeks, or even months, of consistent water time in good learning conditions. Although nothing can beat real time on the water, this book can tell you what to expect before you hit the waves, how to take full advantage of your first session in the water, and what to work on for your next session.

Learning to surf is a mixture of respect, timing, balance, boldness, and humility, with bits of pure elation thrown into the mix. As a beginning surfer, you learn something new every time you go out. Even if you have only a few hours to give it a try, and only manage to belly-ride a 1-foot-high wave, surfing can still be a worthwhile experience. And once you stand up and start gliding across a wave, the fun factor increases exponentially.

A Word on Safety

There's the standard disclaimer in the beginning of this book releasing the author, publisher, and distributor from any liability in case of sunburn, shark attack, jellyfish in swimsuits, dismemberment, death, and just plain drowning. This warning is worth reemphasizing here.

The ocean is the Boss. The ocean can seem playful at times and angry at other times, but ultimately it is completely uncaring about whether or not you get hurt. Don't expect Mother Ocean to send emissaries of graceful dolphins to rescue you if you get caught in a rip current or lose your board. If you are not sure you should go out, that's a giant red neon sign that you shouldn't go out. The waves are always bigger when you're out there. It is better to be on the shore wishing you

were in those waves than in those waves wishing you were on shore.

Although it is always best to surf with someone else for safety, don't rely on the lifeguard or your surf buddy to rescue you. You are ultimately on your own. Unlike other sports such as rock climbing, mountain biking, or skiing, with surfing it can be extremely hard for other folks to notice you're in trouble, get to you in time, and do something when they get there. Reading this book is no substitute for taking surfing lessons, checking conditions before you go out, and surfing within your limits.

Surfing is a full-immersion watersport. Even though you expect to spend most of your time on or connected to your board, it is just as important to know what to do when you are off or separated from your board. Strong swimming and ocean skills are critical. The best way to strengthen your swimming skills is first in a pool and then under calm conditions in open water.

Having said all that, water is pretty soft and forgiving. You should not be overly afraid of wiping out or getting tossed around, because that is where the real learning occurs.

See you in the water!

Surfing, Surfboards, and Surfers

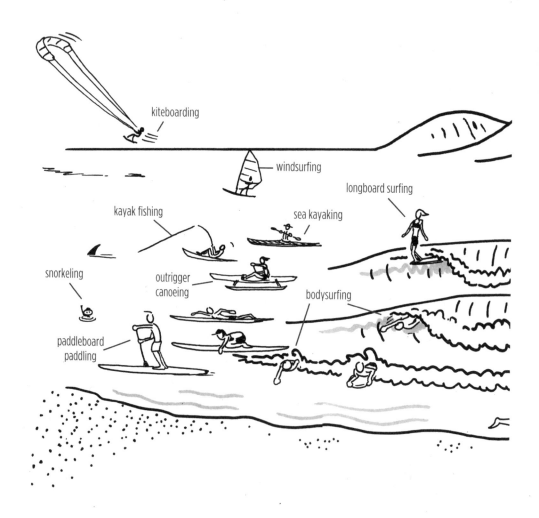

kiteboarding

windsurfing

longboard surfing

kayak fishing

sea kayaking

snorkeling

outrigger
canoeing

bodysurfing

paddleboard
paddling

No matter what your interests or abilities, the coast can be a fantastic playground. First and foremost is surfing with a surfboard. Surfing can also mean sliding any type of craft (a surfboard, boogie board, or even just your body) down the face of a wave. But if the waves are too small for surfing, you can still go for a swim, paddle a paddleboard, outrigger canoe, or sea kayak, or go fishing. If the wind is too strong for surfing, you can try sailing, boardsailing, or kiteboarding. If the water visibility

> "Listen: when someone tells me he or she wants to learn the athleticism, the art, of surfing, my first reaction is invariably, 'careful, it can change everything.'"
>
> —Allan C. Weisbecker, *In Search of Captain Zero*

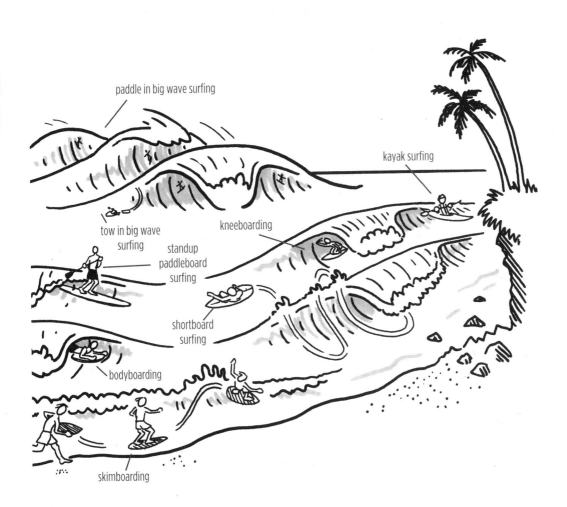

paddle in big wave surfing

kayak surfing

tow in big wave surfing

kneeboarding

standup paddleboard surfing

shortboard surfing

bodyboarding

skimboarding

is good, you can go snorkeling or scuba diving. If the waves are too big, there is always shell collecting, relaxing, sand castle construction and demolition with the kids, as well as sex on the beach (the cocktail, that is). The more watersports you try, the better an overall surfer you become. The most respected surfers are proficient in a wide variety of surfing, from bodysurfing to outrigger canoe surfing to kiteboarding. **So with all these other options, why surf? Because it's simply the most fun you can have.**

HOW SURFING WORKS

To really appreciate surfing, it helps to understand a little bit about the physics of what's going on.

Gravity Sports: It's All Downhill from Here

Surfing is a gravity sport like downhill skiing or snowboarding, with the added excitement that the entire hill is moving with you. Mere humans are newcomers to the sport of surfing. Dolphins and sea lions are the real experts and can surf waves underwater, and pelicans can surf across the updraft on the face of a cresting wave.

Planing

Most surfboards are not buoyant enough to support an upright person in flatwater without sinking, so how is it that surfers are able to stand up and skim across the surface of a moving wave? The difference between skipping a stone and ploinking a pebble is speed across the surface of the water.

With enough speed, even large objects like water-skiers and jetboats stop plowing through the water and start skimming or planing across the surface.

Instead of using a motor, surfers use the speed generated by gravity as they drop down the slope of a moving wave. Unlike a ski hill, a wave slope can change from too flat to too steep in a few seconds, so timing and placement are critical.

too flat

glide zone
(it will be too steep in a few seconds)

too steep

(A) (B) (C)

Finding the Glide Zone

The **glide zone** is a constantly moving area where it is steep enough (but not too steep) for your surfboard to start planing (surfer B). The idea is to sprint shoreward until the glide zone of a wave appears underneath you. If you stand up too soon, before the wave steepens enough, you will sink like a water-skier behind a boat that has run out of gas (surfer A). If you are trying to catch a wave that is too steep for your surfboard, the surfboard will nosedive, or **pearl**, sending you end over end (surfer C).

Catching Waves

Instead of thinking about catching the wave, think about the wave catching up with you. With practice, you will be able to position yourself so the glide zone appears directly beneath you just as the wave catches up with you.

already paddling

Dropping In

Once you succeed in paddling into the glide zone and standing up (this may take some time), you need to figure out what to do next. If you keep your board pointed straight toward shore, you will speed ahead of the wave into the **flats**, where the avalanche of whitewater behind you will soon catch up. Although making **drops** is great fun, the rides are short, and this routine can become tiring after a while.

glide zone

Uh oh.

fall line straight to the beach

new glide zone

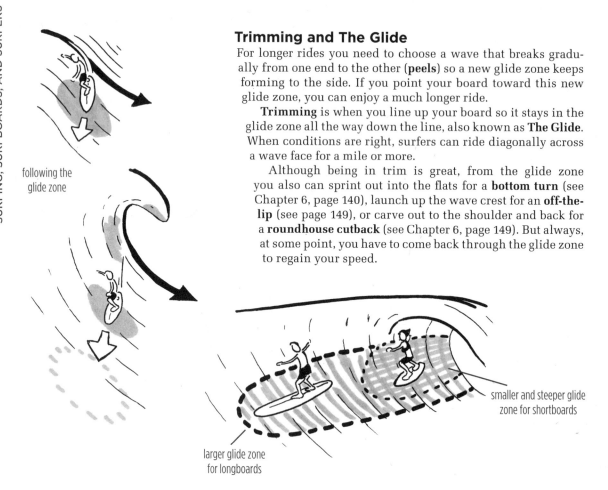

following the
glide zone

Trimming and The Glide

For longer rides you need to choose a wave that breaks gradually from one end to the other (**peels**) so a new glide zone keeps
forming to the side. If you point your board toward this new
glide zone, you can enjoy a much longer ride.

Trimming is when you line up your board so it stays in the
glide zone all the way down the line, also known as **The Glide**.
When conditions are right, surfers can ride diagonally across
a wave face for a mile or more.

Although being in trim is great, from the glide zone
you also can sprint out into the flats for a **bottom turn** (see
Chapter 6, page 140), launch up the wave crest for an **off-the-
lip** (see page 149), or carve out to the shoulder and back for
a **roundhouse cutback** (see Chapter 6, page 149). But always,
at some point, you have to come back through the glide zone
to regain your speed.

smaller and steeper glide
zone for shortboards

larger glide zone
for longboards

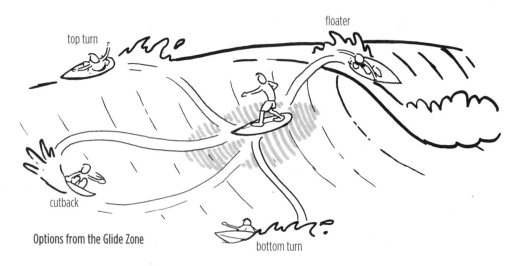

top turn

floater

cutback

bottom turn

Options from the Glide Zone

BEFORE YOU GRAB YOUR SURFBOARD

There are several basic ocean skills you should be comfortable with before you grab a surfboard.

Swim Practice

Even though you may plan on doing all your stroking while on a surfboard, you need to be comfortable swimming in the ocean without a surfboard in case you become separated from your surfboard. Although you don't have to be an Olympic swimmer to surf (but it helps!), you should be able to swim in a pool for at least thirty minutes and tread water for twenty minutes without difficulty. It is perfectly okay to take a touch-up swim lesson to improve your efficiency.

Once your flutter kick is fluttering and your crawl is more than crawling, you should gain some experience swimming in the ocean next to the shore in mild conditions. In general, though, places to surf don't make good places to swim. So before you go, read Chapter 2 about rip currents and check with a lifeguard for recommendations!

Dealing with Waves by Ducking (and Not Diving)

Once you've found a good swimming spot, the next step is to become comfortable with the ins and outs of the shore break. The shore break can change from a Class I to a Class V rapid and back again in just a few seconds, so time your entry and exit to avoid the waves. As you wade out and encounter an oncoming wave, you can either stand sideways on your tiptoes to pass through it, duck under it, or just act like a tourist and let it smack you. Once the water is too deep or the waves are too big to wade through, the safest option is to duck underwater and swim under the turbulence. If you choose to, you can do a low-speed, sinking belly flop and then swim to the bottom. Never dive if there might be any obstacles (such as the bottom) to bump into with your head or torso.

never dive into unknown waters

belly flop— shallow dive

duck

tiptoe

Swimming in Open Water

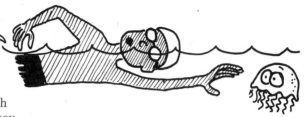

Now that you are beyond the shore break, take a moment to float, relax, and get a sense of the circular motion of passing waves. As you float next to the beach, you will feel a surge toward shore alternating with a backwash away from shore. Predicting these motions is key to getting in and out of the water safely with your surfboard. Take note of any drifting from long-shore currents.

Swimming in the sea is radically different from swimming in a lap pool. For a workout, swim along the shoreline just past the breaking waves. If there is a current along the beach, start by swimming against the current (think of it as a treadmill). Keep your head down and your body level to make progress through the chop and splashes, because swimming with your head up the whole time is slower and not energy efficient. Do lift your head occasionally and look around to keep track of your position. As always, be aware of rip currents (see Chapter 2).

Bodysurfing

pick a gently spilling wave

kick your feet up

hands out front

Bodysurfing is an ideal way to get a feel for waves and develop some coastal coping mechanisms without having to worry about your own surfboard beating you up. Bodysurfing is also a critical skill for aspiring watermen and -women. In the days before surfboards had leashes, when surfers lost their boards they would have to bodysurf back to the beach to retrieve them.

Start in small, gentle waves (less than 3 feet high) that are breaking over a sandy bottom. Instead of a Hawaii 5-o tubing wave, look for gently spilling waves. Avoid bodysurfing in the shore break where waves (and bodies) break directly onto the beach. Select a place where waves are breaking farther offshore for a longer and safer ride.

Ideally, you begin bodysurfing by standing waist to chest deep on a sandbar just a few feet seaward of where the waves break. When a particularly auspicious wave appears and starts to tug your body seaward, push yourself off the bottom toward shore and start swimming aggressively. As the wave lifts you up and surges you forward, take a few more strokes and then extend both hands in front of you as you accelerate down the wave. Go as far as you can, then wade or swim back out and do it again. If you misjudge the wave and feel that it is going to pile-drive your body into the bottom, curl up and cup your hands over your head.

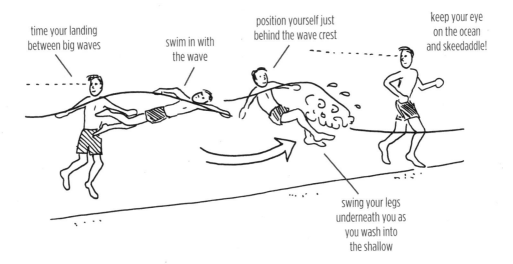

time your landing between big waves

swim in with the wave

position yourself just behind the wave crest

keep your eye on the ocean and skeedaddle!

swing your legs underneath you as you wash into the shallow

Exiting Gracefully

Even if it looks as though you can simply swim toward shore and stand up in the shallows, always look over your shoulder to make sure there isn't a sneaker set of waves heading your way. If there is some wave action coming, stop short of the shore break and wait for a lull between waves. If there is a small surge to deal with, you can swim in with the incoming swell. As you reach the beach, swing your feet underneath you and stand up as the wave surges up the beach. To come in with a breaking wave, swim in at or just behind the wave crest so it crashes in front of you and doesn't dash you into the sand. As you ride the surge in, put your landing gear down as before. Exit quickly, before the receding water washes you back out, and keep an eye out for the next wave.

DIFFERENT TYPES OF SURFING

The most respected surfers are proficient in a wide variety of surfing, from bodysurfing to outrigger canoe surfing. A surf-riding craft needs to be able to do two things: catch a wave, and go where you want to go once you're on the wave. Some craft, such as sea kayaks, make it easy to catch a wave, but it's a clumsy ride. Others, such as short surfboards, are incredibly maneuverable but make it hard to catch a wave. The main focus of this book is on longboards, because they make it easy to catch a wave and are maneuverable enough to turn when you need them to.

Advanced Bodysurfing

Advanced bodysurfers use their shoulders and chest to carve across the face of a wave. Bodysurfers use specialized swim fins—shorter and stiffer than snorkeling fins—so they can catch waves in deep water. **Fin keepers** are miniature leashes that keep the fins attached to your ankles, and fin socks or booties keep your feet nicely padded from blisters. Because walking onshore with fins is problematic, you have to either walk backward or put your fins on and take them off when you are in the water. Some bodysurfers also use a handboard to skim across the surface more easily. It is even possible for skilled bodysurfers to surf a wave underwater the way dolphins do.

Bodyboarding and Kneeboarding

Bodyboards (sometimes called boogie boards) are short, soft foam boards that are four feet long or less. Body boards are the perfect entry into the world of waves for folks who already have strong swimming skills but may not be up for wrestling with a surfboard quite yet. Boogie boards and bodyboards are no longer just toys for little kids and wanna-be surfers. Proficient boogie boarders have as much as or more fun out there than anyone and are masters of insane take-offs and deep barrels. Because they don't have to worry about wiping out while trying to stand up, they can start surfing immediately upon catching a wave. While beginner bodyboarders can have fun without fins, experienced bodyboarders always use fins to help propel themselves. Use the same gradual approach as when learning to surf with a surfboard. A decent bodyboard will have a slick bottom with hardened rails and a leash that attaches to your wrist or upper arm.

Kneeboards are super-short and stubby surfboards that surfers kneel on to better squeeze into tubes. Although kneeboarding is not nearly as popular as it once was, the short but wide board design has been adapted for standup surfing.

kneeboarder tucked into a tight tube

Kayak Surfing

Because of their faster hull speed and paddle propulsion, kayaks can catch waves more easily than surfboards, necessitating great restraint by a kayaker to avoid being a wave hog. In the past, kayakers had a bad reputation for ignoring surf etiquette, but today's kayakers are generally better informed and more neighborly. Kayak surfing is a good alternative if the waves are mushy or choppy, but kayaks are generally not as maneuverable as surfboards in steep waves and advanced conditions.

Surf kayaks have a long hull with a low-volume stern designed to catch and ride ocean waves.

Shorter river kayaks are slower but are popular for doing tricks on a wave face and in whitewater. Sea kayaks excel in small, gentle surf or swells but are the least maneuverable of kayaks. **Wave skis** are high-performance sit-on-top surfboards.

Landing and launching in the surf zone is more complicated in a kayak than on a surfboard and can lead to some hugely entertaining wipeouts. For more information on kayak surfing, check out my book *Sea Kayaking Illustrated* (International Marine/McGraw-Hill, 2003).

surf kayak designed for fast ocean waves

river playboat doing tricks in the soup

wave ski doing a floater

Skimboarding

Skimboards are oval-shaped, flat, finless boards designed to plane across the beach on the thin film of water from a receding wave. Skimboarders toss the board in front of them onto the retreating wave, run after it, jump on it, and ride it out into an oncoming wave, then ride the wave back to shore, somehow without ending up flat on their backs and in traction.

Sailboarding

Sailboarding (also known as **boardsailing** or **windsurfing**) is still a popular sport. Equipment has evolved dramatically from large, stable boards to high-performance wave-carving boards. Most boardsailing is done independently of surfable waves, although skilled riders surf on everything from wind chop to big waves.

Kitesurfing or Kiteboarding

Kitesurfing, or **kiteboarding**, is a cross between windsurfing and wakeboarding, with a little hang gliding thrown in with gusts of wind. Kiteboards are short compared with other boards, and are more similar to wakeboards than surfboards. As with windsurfing, the board is wind- instead of wave-driven, but waves can serve as ramps for aerial maneuvers.

Paddleboard Paddling

Like a road bike or a sea kayak, paddleboards are made to go fast on long-distance journeys rather than to make quick maneuvers. Although paddlers might catch a wind swell on a downwind run from time to time, surfing itself is not a major goal. Instead, surfers use paddleboards for exercising, touring, or racing. Paddleboard paddlers may alternate between lying prone and kneeling to use different muscle groups.

Only 13 miles to go!

Standup Paddleboard Surfing

Standup paddleboards are the perfect choice when you have a long paddle out to a gentle, peeling long-board break. Standup paddleboard, or SUP, surfing is a revitalization of a Hawaiian beachboy trick to stay dry while taking close-up photos of tourists surfing at Waikiki. Paddleboards are propelled by a long canoe paddle wielded by a standing surfer. Surfers also use the paddle to help carve turns while surfing, compensating for the greater weight and length of the board.

Surfers use a parallel skier-style stance when paddling and a sideways snowboard or surfer stance when riding waves. Because of their greater ease in catching waves, standup paddleboard surfers need to exercise restraint with other surfers. Other surfers call SUP surfers "sweepers," "janitors," or "gondoliers." Surfers also take out standup paddleboards on flat days for touring and exercise. Standup paddleboards can provide a great workout on calm days with no surf. More and more folks are using them on inland waterways as well. Think of it as sea kayaking with a better view and dry shorts (until the wind picks up, that is). The trick is to bend your knees a bit more than you think you need to.

While SUP paddling on flat water is easy to pick up, SUP surfing is not. Even for those who can already surf, trying to ride a standup paddleboard in waves for the first time is a humiliating experience. Standup paddleboards are even more unwieldy than longboards, and you also have an expensive paddle to keep track of, so it is best to learn the basics on a soft surfboard, or spongeboard, first.

parallel "skier" stance when paddling

tip of blade angled forward

sideways "snowboarder" or surfing stance when riding a wave

Shortboard Surfing

Shortboards are hyper-maneuverable and lend themselves to slash-and-rip riding styles similar to riding a BMX bike, paddling a playboat, or riding a snowboard at a half-pipe or terrain park. Shortboards can surf steeper waves, take later drops, and carve sharper turns than standard longboards.

Big-Wave Surfing

Big-wave surfing is an entirely different sport, similar to snowboarding in front of an avalanche or kayaking over waterfalls. Because large waves travel so fast, it is hard to paddle fast enough to catch them on a standard surfboard.

There are two radically different approaches to deal with this. Traditional big-wave surfers use long, fast, and narrow **big-wave guns** to paddle into these enormous waves. Tow-in surfers team up with a driver on a personal watercraft who slingshots them down the face, making catching and riding these waves much easier. Tow-in surfing is a team sport with surfers taking turns driving the personal watercraft. Because there is no need for a long surfboard to catch a wave and the wave gives the surfer tremendous speed, tow-in big-wave surfers can use much shorter and more maneuverable surfboards. These boards actually have to be weighted to prevent them from skipping too much. (The personal watercraft also has a safety sled for rescues.)

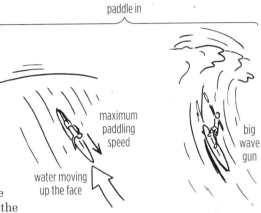

paddle in

maximum paddling speed

water moving up the face

big wave gun

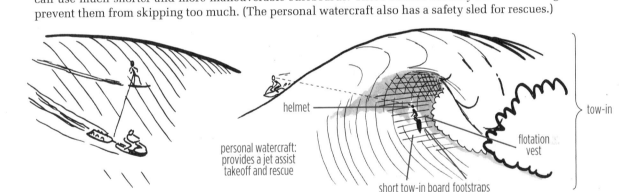

helmet

personal watercraft: provides a jet assist takeoff and rescue

short tow-in board footstraps

flotation vest

tow-in

Longboard Surfing

So if all these other types of surfing are so fun, why even mess with **longboarding**? Well, longboards provide the perfect balance between wave-catching efficiency and wave-riding maneuverability. Longboards are not just for beginners. They are the perfect tool for zen-like glides across wave faces, soulful carves, and cross-steps for noseriding, the utterly cool sensation of walking on water. Longboards excel at catching waves early (farther from shore), and riding smallish and mushy waves. Of all the types of surfing, longboarding is best suited for beginning surfers and is the main focus of this book.

noseriding

SURFBOARDS

The surfboard family tree includes a complex web of classic styles, cutting-edge shapes, revolutions, resurgences, and cross-pollination from other sports. Surfboard evolution has progressed from long and heavy (20 feet and 150 pounds) to shorter and lighter (5 feet and 5 pounds), but recently there has been a resurgence of longboards made of lightweight materials and retro fish or fish-shaped boards. Just as golfers use different clubs for different purposes, experienced surfers choose from a "quiver" of boards depending on their mood and the surf conditions. Nowadays there is a surfboard to fit everyone's ability and style, from potato-chip shortboards to standup paddleboards and everything in between. This is a great time to be a surfer.

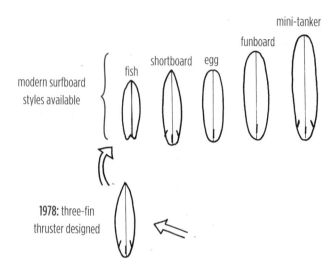

modern surfboard styles available

fish shortboard egg funboard mini-tanker

1978: three-fin thruster designed

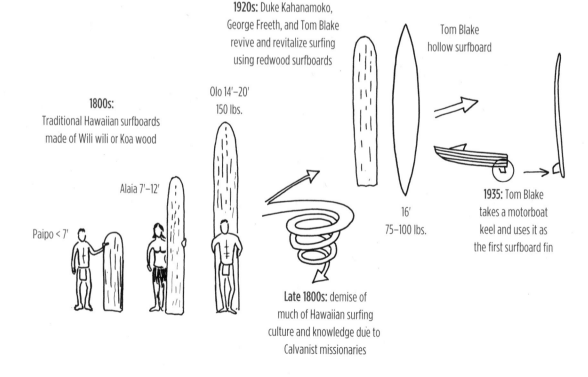

1800s:
Traditional Hawaiian surfboards made of Wili wili or Koa wood

Paipo < 7'

Alaia 7'–12'

Olo 14'–20'
150 lbs.

1920s: Duke Kahanamoko, George Freeth, and Tom Blake revive and revitalize surfing using redwood surfboards

Tom Blake hollow surfboard

16'
75–100 lbs.

1935: Tom Blake takes a motorboat keel and uses it as the first surfboard fin

Late 1800s: demise of much of Hawaiian surfing culture and knowledge due to Calvanist missionaries

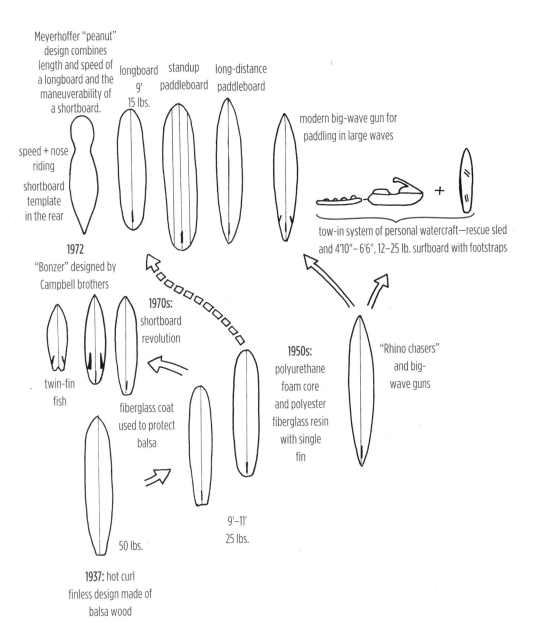

Meyerhoffer "peanut" design combines length and speed of a longboard and the maneuverability of a shortboard.

speed + nose riding

shortboard template in the rear

1972

longboard
9'
15 lbs.

standup paddleboard

long-distance paddleboard

modern big-wave gun for paddling in large waves

tow-in system of personal watercraft—rescue sled and 4'10"–6'6", 12–25 lb. surfboard with footstraps

"Bonzer" designed by Campbell brothers

1970s: shortboard revolution

twin-fin fish

fiberglass coat used to protect balsa

1950s: polyurethane foam core and polyester fiberglass resin with single fin

"Rhino chasers" and big-wave guns

9'–11'
25 lbs.

50 lbs.

1937: hot curl finless design made of balsa wood

Surfboard Anatomy and Design

Plan. The **plan**, or outline, of a surfboard is similar to the frame of a bike. Shortboards are like BMX bikes, longboards are like cruiser bikes, and paddleboards are like road bikes. The plan (skinny, pointy, rounded, wide) helps determine how a surfboard will catch waves, plane, track, and turn.

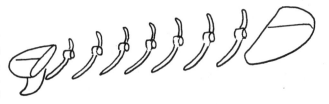

Length. The longer the surfboard, the faster you can paddle it. The faster you can paddle, the easier it is to catch a wave and get the added speed you need to start planing down the face.

With a longboard, you can stand up when a wave first starts to steepen and well before it breaks. With a shortboard you need to wait until the wave crest starts to break, and then you need to stay in the steeper section.

Ironically, once you catch a wave, the shorter the board, the quicker and easier it is to maneuver. Although hull length is helpful for catching

a wave, all that wetted surface area creates a lot of added drag when planing. Because shortboards have less drag when planing as well as much less mass to swing around, they are much faster and more maneuverable than longboards on a wave. This is partly why longboards make gentle, graceful turns and shortboards can make much more aggressive turns.

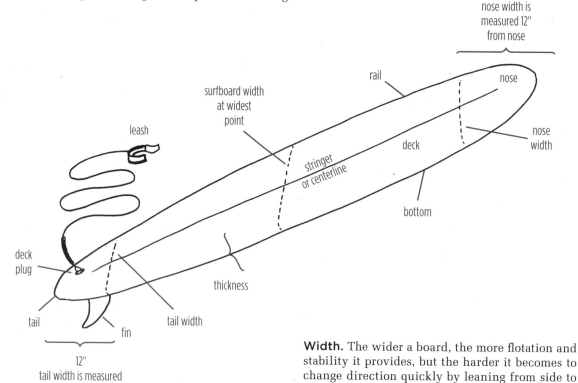

Width. The wider a board, the more flotation and stability it provides, but the harder it becomes to change direction quickly by leaning from side to side.

Foil, or thickness, through the length. Foil, or thickness, helps determine the strength, flotation, and weight of a board. Thickness is measured by calipers at the thickest point, usually in the middle of the board at the widest point. In addition to being easy to paddle, boards with lots of flotation can start planing at slow speeds when the slope of the wave isn't steep. These boards can catch smaller waves, mushier waves, and regular waves sooner than thinner boards with the same plan. Overly buoyant boards are harder to maneuver, however. Your starting board should have enough flotation to float you completely out of the water as you lie on the board.

lots of flotation　　　not enough flotation

Rocker. Rocker describes how much upturn the nose, body, and tail of a board have and helps determine how maneuverable a board is as well as how fast it is. The less rocker a board has, the faster it is when trying to catch a wave, but the more likely the board will nosedive, or pearl, on a steep takeoff. In addition, the more rocker a board has, the sharper a turn the board can make as it follows the shape of the arc.

Pant!

too much rocker

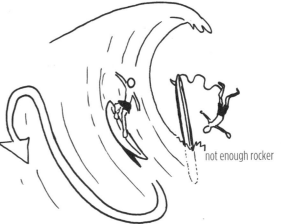

not enough rocker

Bottom shape. The bottom of a surfboard can be convex, concave, V-shaped, flat, carved with channels, or a mixture of these throughout the length of the board. Surfers select a combination according to the size of wave they want to ride and the types of turns they want to make. Talk with your local surfboard shaper to find out more about what might work best for you.

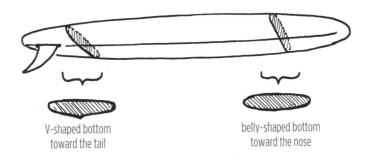

V-shaped bottom
toward the tail

belly-shaped bottom
toward the nose

Nose. In addition to contributing to the overall length of a surfboard, the width of a **nose** helps determine the board's planing speed. The wider the nose, the greater the board's surface area and the more easily it will catch a wave. The narrower the nose, the quicker the board will turn and the less wind resistance it will impose when you're trying to catch a wave against a stiff offshore breeze.

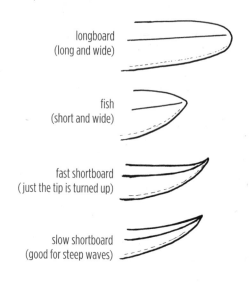

longboard
(long and wide)

fish
(short and wide)

fast shortboard
(just the tip is turned up)

slow shortboard
(good for steep waves)

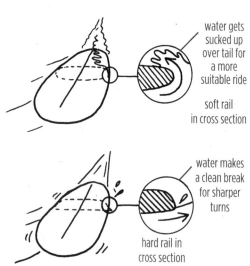

water gets sucked up over tail for a more suitable ride

soft rail in cross section

water makes a clean break for sharper turns

hard rail in cross section

Rail. The **rail** is a cross section of the edge of a board. As with skis or a kayak, sharper or highly angled rails tend to give higher performance but are less forgiving, and softer or round rails tend to be less reactive and more forgiving.

Tail. The surface area in the tail of a board determines how well it will maneuver at slower speeds; the wider the tail, the more maneuverable it is at slow speeds. For fast waves, though, you want a narrow tail that won't slow you down with a lot of surface area. Differently shaped tails are designed to either grab and track across a wave face or slide across it for a looser ride. Square tails, squash tails, and round tails all have a lot of surface area that provides greater planing area and looseness on a wave. Pin tails and rounded pin tails provide a longer rail length and make it easier to hold a line on steep, hollow waves without skidding out. **Swallowtails** provide the advantages of wide and narrow tails.

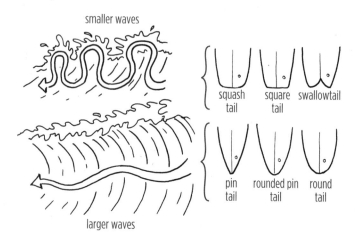

smaller waves

squash tail   square tail   swallowtail

pin tail   rounded pin tail   round tail

larger waves

Fins. Let's say you're at the top of a snow-covered hill with that infamous, ankle-breaking tree at the bottom. A plastic saucer, cafeteria tray, or inner tube is great for going straight down the hill and into the tree. If you want to angle across the hill and miss the tree, however, you will need to ride something with edges (skis or a snowboard) that can catch the snow and redirect your downward slide off to the side. Surfing is similar.

steering

no steering

A raft or surf mat is fine for going straight down the wave, over the tourists, and straight up the beach, but at some point you are going to want to angle across the wave for a longer, better, more controlled ride.

If you try to angle a finless plank across a wave, the back of the board will spin out, also known as **sliding ass**. A surfboard **fin** keeps the tail from sliding out and provides forward drive.

Problems with a finless surfboard.

steeper = faster

less steep = slower

Whoa!

"sliding ass"

Just as the sideways swipe of a shark's tail drives the shark forward, your fin converts the sideways force of your tail sliding down the wave face into forward thrust to propel you across the wave face.

sideways pressure on fin = forward thrust or drive

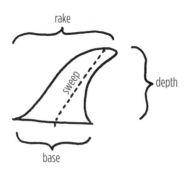

rake

sweep

depth

base

As with surfboard shapes, fins need to provide a balance between going straight and turning. Deeper fins with a larger surface area create more forward drive and prevent the tail from sliding out, but they also make it harder to execute sharp turns. Smaller fins allow sharp turns and give the board a looser feel. A longer fin base, greater **rake** (how far back the fin tip goes), and greater **sweep** (how far the deepest part is angled back from the midline of the base) all mean greater forward drive and wider turns. Fins that have little sweep or rake or are moved forward on the surfboard allow for sharper turns.

There are fin designs, shapes, and combinations for every condition. Many longboards have a single, deep fin that keeps a good grip on the wave yet allows smooth turns. "**Quad**" surfboards have four fins, while **fish** often have two. The majority of modern surfboards have a **thruster** setup with a center fin at the back and two smaller side fins that still bite the water if the board is on edge or on a steep wave. The side fins are toed in, which helps when carving turns.

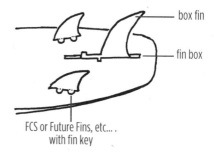

box fin

fin box

FCS or Future Fins, etc... .
with fin key

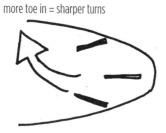

more toe in = sharper turns

It is possible to be cut by surfboard fins, sometimes severely, making board control a priority. Surfco makes safety fins with rubber edges that help prevent lacerations. These fins are available in a variety of models that fit most surfboards, so you can easily replace standard hard fins with these softer-edged fins.

side fin still grabs
the water when cutting
across steep wave

Single Fin Box Found on Longboards

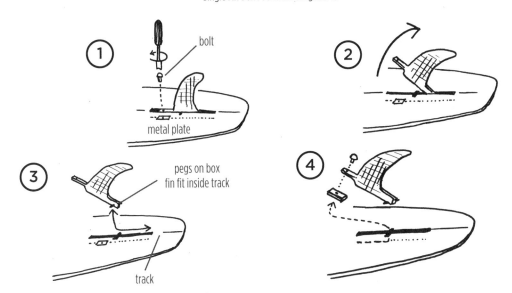

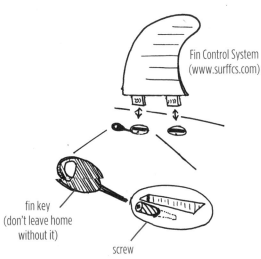

Some fins are glassed in or permanently mounted, while others are removable, a feature that is helpful for traveling and for switching fins for different conditions. Older surfboards and many longboards have fin boxes along the stringer at the tail of the board. The fin box has a horizontal track or slot running inside it. Box fins (that fit in the fin box) have a horizontal pin at one end of the fin base and a horizontal metal plate with a bolt at the other end. These two anchor points fit in the track.

You can slide a box fin forward or backward by loosening the bolt. Move the fin forward for shorter turns, back for longer turns, and in the middle for a balance.

To remove a box fin, turn the board upside down and unscrew the bolt at the front or back of the fin from the metal plate set inside the track. Lift this end of the fin out of the fin box, keeping track of the metal plate. Slide the other end of the fin with the pin until you can fit it through the wider opening in the middle of the fin box. To reinstall, insert the metal plate in the track and slide it underneath where the bolt will be, then reinsert the fin, pin first.

Modern high-performance fins, such as the FCS (Fin Control Systems) and Future Fins, use a different method in which small angled screws hold the fins in place. You need a fin key or an Allen wrench to unscrew the screws far enough to remove, replace, or insert fins. Screw only hand tight. If you are having trouble unscrewing the screws, try a new Allen wrench before taking the board to a surfboard repair shop.

Removing a Box Fin from a Fin Box on a Futures Fin System (www.futuresfins.com)

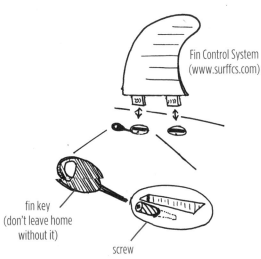

Fin Control System (www.surffcs.com)

fin key (don't leave home without it)

screw

FCS, Future Fins, and others use a fin key

Putting it all together. Although longboards and shortboards often represent opposite ends of the spectrum for each design feature, some hybrid surfboard designs mix features of the two. For example, fish-shaped surfboards follow the shortboard template but incorporate some of a longboard's width and thickness for easier planing in smaller waves. Funboards, mini-tankers, and egg-shaped surfboards are different types of cross-breeds based on a longboard template but made shorter to increase maneuverability.

The Meyerhoffer hourglass design incorporates the speed of a paddleboard for catching waves, the stability of a longboard for noseriding when standing on the front half, and the turning ability of a shortboard when standing at the rear half.

For beginners, start with the longest and widest board you can reasonably carry (from 8' to 9'6").

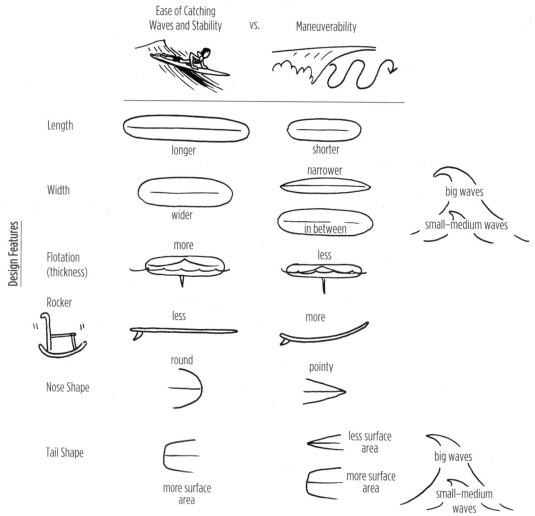

Performance Results

Surfboard Materials and Shaping

Think of surfboards as superhero Styrofoam cups able to dash down enormous waves without getting their foam wet. The rigid foam that makes surfboards so light and buoyant would normally become water-logged and disintegrate in the sea. The secret is that the foam is wrapped in resin-cured fiberglass cloth, which gives surfboards their strength and imper-meability. The foam core also has a wooden **stringer** running down the center for structural stability.

In what may seem like a deliberate effort to con-fuse nonsurfers with obscure manufacturing termi-nology, surfboards are classified according to the resin used to harden the fiberglass. Polyester or traditional boards use a polyester resin around a polyurethane (PU) foam core, while epoxy boards use an epoxy resin around a polystyrene foam core. Surfers refer to the resin because applying the wrong resin to the wrong type of foam will melt the foam into a pile of toxic goo.

Foam blanks come either preshaped or as an unshaped slab that can be carved by an experi-enced shaper or a machine to exact specifications. Two layers of 4- or 6-ounce fiberglass cloth are applied on the foam deck, with one layer on the bot-tom. The appropriate laminating resin then bonds the floppy fiberglass cloth to the foam and cures to form a hard protective coating. Additional layers of surface resin and colors are then applied to finish the board. Because of the toxic materials used in construction, surfboard shapers use respirators and other safety equipment.

If you are interested in learning more, it is defi-nitely worth asking for a tour of the shaping room at your local surf shop. If you are interested in shap-ing your own surfboard, I recommend reading the classic *Essential Surfing* by George Orbelian.

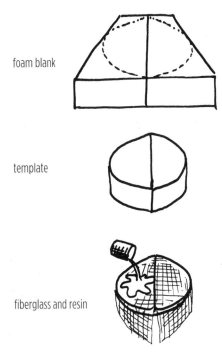

foam blank

template

fiberglass and resin

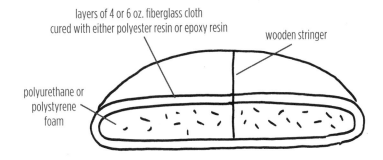

layers of 4 or 6 oz. fiberglass cloth
cured with either polyester resin or epoxy resin

wooden stringer

polyurethane or
polystyrene
foam

Soft surfboards. Soft surfboards, sometimes called **spongeboards**, are the best choice for beginners. These wide, stable boards are virtually indestructible and are more forgiving if you and your board exchange love taps in the surf. Sponge surfboards are different from polyester or epoxy boards in that they have a spongy outer layer surrounding a stiffer closed-cell foam core.

The foam top provides a good grip so you don't need to wax the deck. Consider wearing a rash guard and board shorts to protect your skin from spongeboard decks that have been scuffed up and feel rough. The speed and turning ability of these boards are fairly limited, so once you can consistently stand up and start angling along the face of a wave, you may want to move to a higher performance surfboard.

a pod of beginning surfers practicing with soft surfboards

Soft-top surfboards. Soft-tops are epoxy surfboards with a thin layer of foam padding on the deck and rails. Although billed as "soft," the layer of padding on these boards is significantly less than that of sponge surfboards. The hard bottom of these boards does provide better performance. These boards are a fine choice to move up to when you want a little more control for angling across a wave, but a foam surfboard is still better to start with.

Where's my surfboard?

Polyester-resin/polyurethane (PU) foam surfboards. Polyester-resin/polyurethane (PU) **foam surfboards** are high-performance boards that are used around the world. Their downside is that fiberglass hardened with polyester resin is more susceptible to dings if the board comes into contact with a knee, doorway, ceiling fan, or pavement. In addition, both the foam and resin are toxic for shapers to work with. Polyester-resin surfboards are not the most user-friendly boards so you should be ready for a few dings on your board or body.

Epoxy-resin/polystyrene foam surfboards. Epoxy-resin/polystyrene foam surfboards are more durable high-performance boards and make a good all-around choice for intermediate and advanced surfers. The core of epoxy boards is made from polystyrene, and the fiberglass covering is hardened with extremely durable epoxy resin. Because this foam is quite light, the boards are very buoyant and can feel "corky."

There are two basic types of polystyrene foam. Expanded polystyrene foam (EPS) is composed of little pellets like those found in cheap Styrofoam coolers from convenience stores. EPS foam is inexpensive but will absorb water rapidly through a ding. Extruded polystyrene foam (XTR) is a closed-cell foam and won't absorb as much water, but it is much more expensive. Epoxy-resin boards are a good rental choice for intermediate and advanced surfers because of their durability and high performance. In addition, the resin and foam are far less toxic than polyester-resin/polyurethane boards, and polystyrene foam is even recyclable.

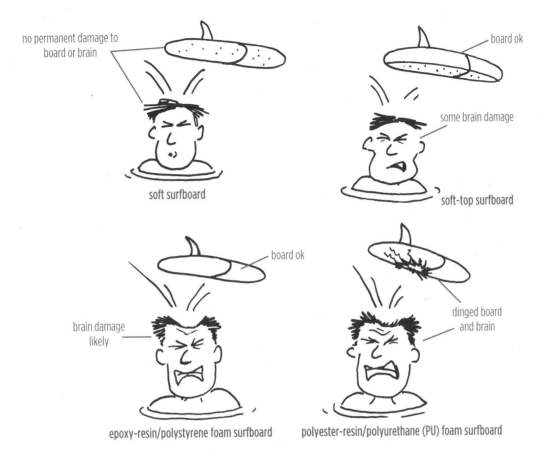

no permanent damage to board or brain

soft surfboard

board ok

some brain damage

soft-top surfboard

board ok

brain damage likely

epoxy-resin/polystyrene foam surfboard

dinged board and brain

polyester-resin/polyurethane (PU) foam surfboard

"Black Monday," The Day Clark Foam Shut Its Doors

Clark Foam for decades was the world's largest producer of polyurethane blanks, producing thousands of surfboard blanks a day. After increasing pressure from state and federal regulatory agencies and concerns about carcinogens, Clark Foam suddenly closed its doors on December 5, 2005, leaving surfboard shapers with a limited supply of foam blanks. The wave of panic that spread through the surf industry was covered in the national and international media.

Many surfboard shapers who ran small businesses on tight budgets were hard-pressed to find alternative supplies of foam blanks. Surfboard manufacturers, such as Surftech and Patagonia, who produce higher priced but more environmentally friendly polystyrene blanks, are taking advantage of the increase in business. Meanwhile, other traditional polyurethane surf blank companies are filling the void using similar materials and manufacturing. It remains to be seen whether the surf industry capitalizes on this opportunity to become more environmentally responsible.

Choosing a board that's best for you. Regardless of which specialized model most appeals to you, all beginners should start with a spongeboard (see page 30) in a longboard shape and master the basics before investing in a more advanced surfboard.

After you are fairly accomplished on the soft surfboard and want to try a more advanced surfboard, don't jump straight into a shortboard. Instead continue your apprenticeship on a standard longboard. Look for a board 8 feet long or longer and 22 inches wide that is somewhat tailored to your height and weight. Anything over 9 feet 6 inches might be a bit too unwieldy, so don't try to use your old Bic windsurfing board.

You can customize your surfboard with additional safety items such as rubber-edged fins and nose and tail guards from Surfco. These rubber "bumpers" can reduce the severity of injuries should your board tag you or someone else. These safety features are recommended for everyone; they do not compromise performance and they are affordable when compared with a trip to the emergency room.

If you want to move on to a more maneuverable shortboard (which is a different sport entirely), wait until you can consistently catch and ride waves on your longboard. Starting out on a shortboard may seem like a shortcut to radical maneuvers, but you will be a better shortboarder sooner by spending your first season on a longboard.

shortboards may be cool, but start surfing with a longboard

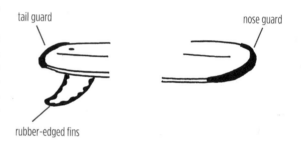

not enough wax

too much wax

Surfboard Necessities and Accessories

Wax. Not to be confused with ski wax applied to the bottom of skis to make them glide on snow, surfboard wax provides traction on the deck. Nothing is more frustrating than wiping out on a perfect wave because you didn't have enough wax on your board. In addition to keeping your feet planted on the board, waxing before you go out provides some much needed time to watch the surf. (The spongy decks of soft surfboards and soft-top surfboards may provide enough grip that they do not need wax.)

Surfers use different types of wax depending on the water temperature. Surfers first apply a hard warm-water wax or paraffin wax for the first layer, or base coat, on a surfboard because it bonds well to the deck and provides a good surface for other layers to adhere to. Surfers then use a top coat that is particularly suited for the water temperature (cold, cool, warm, or tropical water). The colder the water, the softer the wax for increased grip. When soft coldwater wax is used in warm water, it becomes too soft and washes away easily. In cold water, a hard, warm-water wax may harden too much and not provide enough traction. In warm water, a hard base coat can also be used as the top coat. Your local surf shop should be able to set you up with wax suited to wherever you are going.

Store your wax in a sealable plastic bag out of the sun. Growing up, I ruined my mom's car dashboard (twice) with ill-placed bars of Mr. Zog's Sex Wax. Wax can also melt off your surfboard and onto your board bag or board sock. So always put your surfboard in the same way to avoid getting wax on the bottom of your surfboard. Surfers sometimes wear rash guards to ward off wax rash, a potentially debilitating skin abrasion on one's chest from surfboard wax.

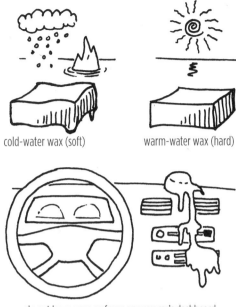

cold-water wax (soft)   warm-water wax (hard)

do not leave your surf wax on your car's dashboard

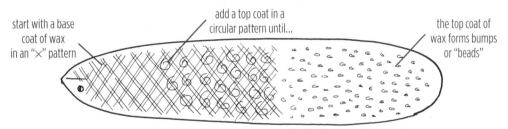

start with a base coat of wax in an "×" pattern

add a top coat in a circular pattern until...

the top coat of wax forms bumps or "beads"

once you have bumps of base coat, add a top coat in a circular pattern for more bumps

To wax a new board, start by making diagonal crosshatch marks on your board with a base coat. Then cover up all shiny gaps by rubbing the wax in a circular motion until tiny beads of base coat

for normal surfing   for noseriding

form. The goal is to "kill" all the shine. You can also place the wax in a paper cup filled with warm water to make the base-coat wax easier to apply.

Coat the area of the deck where you plan to lie on the board. There is no need to wax all the way to the nose unless you want to practicing noseriding. Be sure to wax the rails so you can grab the rails of the board. Once you have covered up all the shiny surfaces with the base coat and made a good base, apply the appropriate top coat in a circular manner. Try to use the entire surface area of the bar of wax, and avoid creating sharp corners in the wax. You know you are doing it right when little bumps of wax start forming. Stop when you have an even coat of bumps across the deck where you will be laying and standing.

Every time you go surfing, you rub off a little bit of the wax. Surfers generally touch up the top coat of wax every time or every other time they head out. Over time you will notice that your wax has become grimy or greasy. A wax comb is a cheap and handy item to have. You can rejuvenate old slippery wax by scraping traction grooves back into it with the tines of that comb before rubbing on new wax.

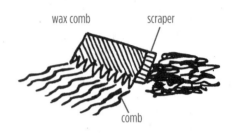

Every few months, you will want to remove all the wax and apply a fresh coat. To remove the wax, use the scraper side of the wax comb (a few minutes in the sun can soften the wax). Once most of the wax is removed, a tool like the Pickle (a mesh bag that helps rub off the wax) is useful for removing any wax remnants. Be sure to properly discard your wax scrapings.

To make sure the wax doesn't melt off your board while you are on the beach, cover the deck with a towel or place your board upside down so the deck is arched above the sand. If you already have a gooey deck of half-melted wax, dunk your board briefly in the water so the wax solidifies before paddling out.

keep your deck out of the sun and sand

Some surfers prefer permanent traction pads glued directly to the deck instead of wax. Traction pads also provide a land-mark for your feet when you stand up, particularly for your rear foot. To apply a traction pad, first remove all the wax.

traction pad

Leashes. Leashes are semi-elastic cords that keep your surfboard nearby when you fall off, saving you a long swim to shore and preventing your board from pummeling people far inside of you or smashing against the rocks. Leashes also keep a fantastic flotation device, your surfboard, nearby if you become tired. Because surfboards are more buoyant than surfers, surfers have been known to climb up their leashes to the surface after deep, tur-bulent wipeouts. More dramatically, leashes have also been used as tourniquets after shark attacks. Although leashes can present some hazards (see below), it is much safer to surf with a leash than

without one. Since leashes do break, you should always be able to swim back to shore without your surfboard. Leashes attach to the ankle of the foot that is closest to the tail of the surfboard. Some longboard leashes attach around the calf instead of the ankle to reduce the chances of tripping while you are walking the nose.

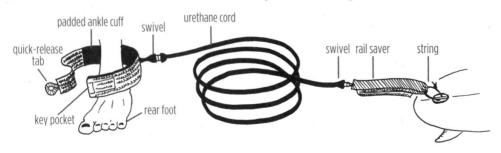

keep your head down after a wipeout

climbing the leash up to the surface after a big wave wipeout

One of the drawbacks of using a leash is that when you wipe out, the whitewater pushes your board toward shore while you stay in place, stretching out your leash. When the wave subsides, your stretched-out leash will sling your surfboard back toward your face just as you are surfacing. Protect your head by always staying underwater for several seconds after you wipe out and always cover your face with your hands and arms when you surface.

Another disadvantage is that leashes encourage the bad habit of ditching surfboards when paddling out through oncoming waves. Instead of holding on to their surfboards and taking a bit of a thrashing, many beginners jettison their boards, dive into the calm water below the whitewater, and rely on their leash (called a **kook cord** in this case) to have their surfboard waiting beside them when they surface. While these surfers are safely beneath the surface, the whitewater converts their surfboards into weapons of mass destruction for anyone nearby. Learn how to hold on to your board at the end of a ride and when paddling out. See Chapter 3 for tips on holding on to your surfboard in the soup.

don't ditch your surfboard

make sure you know where the quick release tab is

A third cautionary note is that leashes can become snagged underwater or on rocks at the shorebreak. The cuff should have a quick-release tab that you should be able to find without looking.

When choosing a leash, look for one with the cord about as long as your surfboard. Also make sure your leash comes with a **rail saver**, a wide strip of webbing that protects the surfboard rail from being damaged by a taut, narrow leash cord. At the end of the rail saver, overlapping hook and loop closures secure a short loop of string tied in a knot. This string is hitched around the bar inside the deck plug.

To disconnect the leash from the surfboard, release these hook-and-loop closures from the string loop.

To secure a new string, tie a new loop with an overhand knot and use a girth hitch to secure it to the deck plug. Make sure the rail saver rests against the rail.

When walking with your surfboard, make sure the leash is not dragging. Make sure the Velcro cuff is clean and not dirty or sandy. On sandy beaches, affix the leash just before you enter the water. Before putting your leash on, make sure it isn't looped in a knot which will become permanent once your leash tightens. The padded cuff

make sure your Velcro closures are secure

tie a simple overhand loop

secure the string around the bar in the deck plug with a girth hitch

wraps around your rear ankle just tightly enough so the cord sticks out to the side, where you are less likely to step on it. If you are getting in and out of surf spots with lots of rocks, pick up all the slack in the leash to minimize snags. In areas with problem snags, another alternative is to put the leash on and take it off in the water once you are past the rocks. To avoid kinking and potentially weakening the leash, store it loosely in your board sock or board bag instead of wrapping it tightly around the tail.

Transporting Your Surfboard

Board socks, board bags, coffins, and hard cases. Many surfers store and transport their surfboards in surfboard socks or more protective board bags to shield them from bumps and sunburn. A surfboard sock is a tube of thin, stretchy fabric that slips over the surfboard nose and down the board and cinches around the tail to provide minimal protection. Board bags, which sandwich a board between two padded sleeves with a zippered opening along the rear half, offer more protection. Like surf socks, board bags are for everyday use. Some board bags have a slot to accommodate the fin. Travel board bags specifically designed for airlines have additional padding and pockets for gear. Coffins are cases that hold multiple surfboards. Solid cases are also available that minimize the

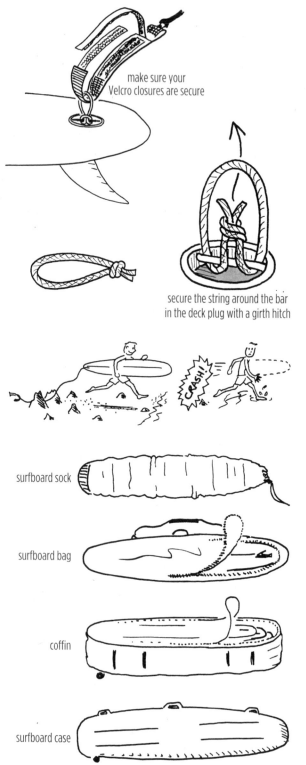

surfboard sock

surfboard bag

coffin

surfboard case

risk of dings. Many airlines now charge per surfboard, so surfers traveling on a budget have to be more selective about which surfboards they bring and which airlines they fly. See Chapter 7 for packing tips.

Because surfboard wax can rub off onto the interior of the board sock or bag, insert your surfboard with the deck facing the same way every time to avoid gumming up the sleek bottom of your surfboard with wax.

bike rack

Bikes and boards. If you are close enough to the beach, biking to the beach eliminates parking hassles, saves gas, and is a sign of a healthy lifestyle. You will see surfers of all ages biking to the beach with their surfboards tucked under their arms and their towels and wetsuits in their backpacks.

If you like to have both hands on the handlebars, several surfboard racks are available that affix to your bike and will even hold longboards. The simplest models consist of a pair of U-shaped bars that affix to a bike frame and secure the surfboard with bungee cords. There are also bike trailers for towing your longboard or standup paddleboard. The outstanding Xtracycle (xtracycle.com) transforms your bike into a sport utility bicycle with a side rack for your longboard and a separate compartment for your wetsuit, towel, and other gear.

tailgate
pads and straps

Cars and trucks. There are racks especially made to secure surfboards on car tops, but most any type of car rack system and cam straps will work. Because surfboards are more fragile than plastic kayaks or snowboards, make sure that there is padding on the crossbars and between any stacked surfboards. If you don't have a board bag for padding, you can use towels or wetsuits as impromptu padding or you can buy specially made padding or make your own from pipe insulation.

Place the longest boards on the bottom. Load the boards upside down to avoid melting the wax and backward so the fins will arrest any backward

slide. If you don't have a board bag or sock to loosely stuff your leash inside, wrap the leash around the tail and close the cuff back on the leash. Use a decent amount of force to secure the straps, but you don't want to hear any creaking or crunching noises. If you are using a cam strap with a metal buckle, position the buckle so it is either on the side in a gap between the surfboard rail and rack or across the overturned bottom of the surfboard (preferably padded). Never place a buckle across the rail. If you have a pickup truck, there are specialized racks that fit over the tailgate to secure longboards.

strap buckles not across surfboard rails

towel or wetsuit for padding

load surfboards upside down and fins first

board bag

padded bars

There are also removable "soft" surf racks that you attach to the car by threading straps through the open doors; separate straps are used for the boards. Soft racks are ideal for plane travel if you plan on taking a taxi or a rental car from the airport to the beach. If you are renting a surfboard, a soft rack will enable you to load a surfboard on the rental car so you can check out other breaks. Be forewarned that rain will drip along the straps and can soak the interior of the car.

Always keep your eye on your surfboards and check the boards regularly. Stop and adjust things if anything appears loose.

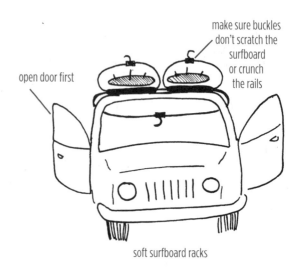

open door first

make sure buckles don't scratch the surfboard or crunch the rails

soft surfboard racks

If there's room, transporting your surfboards inside your car is the most streamlined and secure method. Fully recline the passenger seat and lay the surfboards there. Your surfing buddy can sit behind you. Also check to see if the rear seat opens to the trunk. Never leave your surfboard or body board inside a hot vehicle, though, because heat can warp the internal structure of some boards in addition to melting the wax.

Surfboard locks. Unscrupulous ne'er-do-wells do steal unattended surfboards, so keep a close eye on your board, or buy one of several surfboard locks that attach to the surfboard, fin box, or deck plug and then to your car racks (which also should be locked).

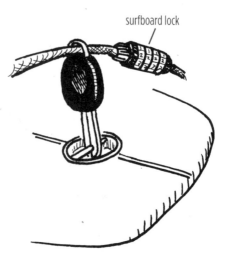

surfboard lock

SURFBOARD CARE AND REPAIR

Handling. For all the abuse surfboards take in the water, they are remarkably fragile. Handle a surfboard as carefully as you would a fluorescent lightbulb tube. Act as though you know what you're doing in the surf shop by balancing boards on the toe of your shoe or sandal when examining them, so they don't touch the hard floor.

Storage. Because salt water is mildly corrosive, rinse off your surfboard and leash with fresh water after every surfing session. Ultraviolet rays can dramatically degrade surfboard materials, so store your board out of the sun in a safe place where it won't get knocked over by the dog or stolen.

Dings. A ding is an owie, usually from an impact with a hard object such as a rock, another surfboard, or your head. Pressure dings are concavities or dents in the deck or the bottom of the surfboard (usually from a knee) where the underlying foam has been crushed like popped bubble wrap but the

fiberglass is still uncracked and laminated to the foam. Pressure dings are the surfboard equivalent of bruises and are usually ignored.

A soft spot is where the overlying fiberglass has separated and become delaminated from the crushed foam beneath it. Soft spots warrant professional repair because the delamination can spread and significantly weaken the board. A buckle is where the fiberglass has delaminated across the deck and stringer—a buckle can cause the board to break in two.

Cracks in the fiberglass are the surfboard equivalent of a laceration and can allow water to seep into the foam like an infection. Waterlogged areas are usually discolored, weigh the board down, and weaken the foam.

Punctures or avulsions are dings where the underlying foam has been crushed and needs to be replaced and refiberglassed.

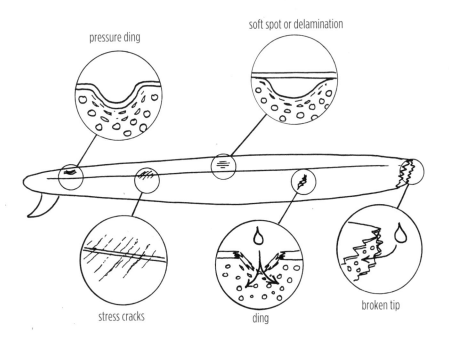

pressure ding

soft spot or delamination

stress cracks

ding

broken tip

Repairs. Plugging a ding with a gob of surfboard wax or covering it with duct tape might serve as a bandage for the rest of the weekend, but any dings where water can get into the foam need to be repaired before the surfboard becomes a submarine or snaps in two.

Surfboard repair shops do a very professional job and can also repair your repair efforts. Be sure to ask for a cost and turnaround estimate because there may be a backlog of several weeks.

You can fix simple dings yourself much more quickly with a ding repair kit purchased from your local surf shop. It is helpful to know what type of resin-foam combination your surfboard is made of so you select the right repair kit (use polyester resin for polyurethane foam and epoxy resin for polystyrene foam; polyester resin will melt polystyrene foam). I recommend Solarez (www.solarez.com) ding repair kits that combine the resin and fiberglass in one tube. Instead of having to add toxic chemicals as a catalyst, sunlight is the hardener.

It is always a good idea to wear protective gloves when handling fiberglass and resin.

First remove any splintered fiberglass and crushed foam and scrape off the wax around the wound. Let the ding dry out completely.

Once the ding is dry, rough up the area around the ding with sandpaper and wipe clean with rubbing alcohol to assure a good bond with the new resin. Mark off this area with masking tape to minimize resin spillage or to help shape the resin/fiberglass mix around a nose or tail. While out of direct sunlight, squeeze some resin/fiberglass mix directly from the tube into the ding, spanning the damaged area and filling up all gaps. Spread the gel around with a popsicle stick. It is ok to have a little bit of overflow.

Next, lay a piece of clear plastic wrap over the repair to smooth out the surface. If you need to, you can gently work the resin in with your fingers by pressing on top of the plastic sheet, squeezing any bubbles out to the side.

When you are ready to harden the Solarez gel, expose the repair to the sun for a few minutes. After the resin cures and is hard to the touch, remove the plastic wrap and sand the patch even with the surfboard surface with fine sandpaper. You are now ready to wax up and go surfing again!

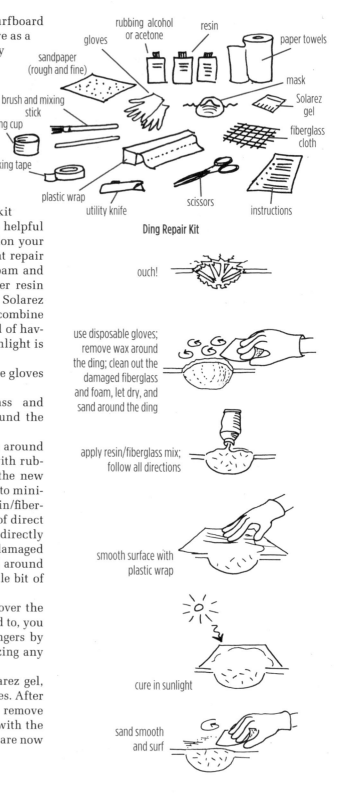

rubbing alcohol or acetone · resin · paper towels · gloves · sandpaper (rough and fine) · mask · brush and mixing stick · Solarez gel · mixing cup · fiberglass cloth · masking tape · plastic wrap · utility knife · scissors · instructions

Ding Repair Kit

ouch!

use disposable gloves; remove wax around the ding; clean out the damaged fiberglass and foam, let dry, and sand around the ding

apply resin/fiberglass mix; follow all directions

smooth surface with plastic wrap

cure in sunlight

sand smooth and surf

WETSUITS AND OTHER WET STUFF

"I love the smell of neoprene in the morning ..."

Wetsuits

Wetsuits, invented by Jack O'Neill in the 1950s, have revolutionized surfing. This invention of neoprene rubber filled with tiny insulating air bubbles has enabled surfers formerly restricted to tropical and seasonally warm waters to expand their surfing into high latitudes year-round. Some of the best surf breaks in the world are now accessible thanks to wetsuits. Wetsuits also offer some added flotation if you're swimming in the soup. Some newer wetsuits are made out of limestone by-products instead of petroleum, making them much more environmentally friendly.

Wetsuits work by allowing a thin layer of water inside the suit that your body warms up to skin temperature (this is why the first dip is always chilly) and by providing a blubber-like layer of insulation from the surrounding water. Ideally, the thin layer of water that your body warms up stays inside the suit. Every time a new wave of water enters your suit, it flushes out the warmed-up water and forces you to start over again with a cold layer. Frequent duck diving, turning turtle, wipeouts, or various thrashings chill you down significantly and shorten your time in the water. Wetsuits should be skin-tight but comfortable and not binding. The better fitting the suit, the faster you will get warm and the warmer you will stay. It is well worth the extra money to buy a well-fitting, high-quality wetsuit.

The thicker the neoprene, the warmer the suit. Wetsuit thickness is measured in millimeters (mm or "mil") with thicker neoprene used in the trunk and thinner neoprene used in the arms, for better mobility. A 2/1 mm wetsuit is good for cool water, a 4/3 mm wetsuit for cold water, and a 5/4 mm suit for frigid water.

Drysuits popular for cold-water scuba diving and kayaking don't work as well in the surf environment because they tend to be baggy and cumbersome when flailing with your board in the waves.

Most surfers go in the buff beneath wetsuits (see the towel trick below), but wearing a swimsuit enables you to struggle into and out of the suit without the added worry of flashing the crowd. One of the less pleasurable tasks in surfing is putting on a wet, cold, sandy wetsuit. To avoid this, always try to rinse, hang, and dry out your wetsuit between outings. Rinse your wetsuit out with fresh water, turn it inside out to dry, and hang on a thick plastic or wooden hanger (or several hangers) between uses to prevent creasing. If the water is truly frigid and you didn't get a chance to dry out your wetsuit between sessions, use a rash guard to buffer the shock. Another alternative is to pre-warm your wet wetsuit with hot water from your house and keep it in a plastic bin or a dry bag for the drive to the beach.

Wetsuits provide good insulation in the water when they are wet, but not such good insulation out of the water. If you take a break on the beach between sessions, stay warm by unpeeling the top half of your wetsuit, drying off with a towel, and putting on a jacket. If it's cold outside, change into dry clothes as soon as you get out of the water.

Although wetsuits are stretchy and relatively durable, you need to treat them well. When getting into or out of a wetsuit, stand on a mat or in a tub to keep the dirt and sand off the wetsuit. This is particularly important in case you don't have a chance to rinse out the wetsuit before your next session. If you think you might be late for whatever you'll be doing after surfing, bring a jug of hot fresh water to rinse off yourself and your wetsuit so you can skip a shower and go directly to work/school/graduation/your wedding.

hot, fresh-water rinse

towel wrap

changing mat

bin to keep wetsuit clean

trying to get out of a wetsuit in a hurry

If you find yourself jumping up and down and straining while putting on or taking off your wetsuit, you are putting too much stress on the suit (and yourself). Be careful not to gouge or rip the neoprene with long fingernails. Follow manufacturer directions (some suits have such a small opening that they require some yoga-like maneuvers) and keep advancing the suit on your body to avoid bunching. Although tears in neoprene can be repaired with Aquaseal or Seam Grip, split seams are best repaired by the manufacturer.

To Pee or Not to Pee?

Peeing in a wetsuit, particularly if you are a little chilled, can transform your clammy wetsuit into your own intimate Jacuzzi, at least for a little while. To avoid a stinky suit (or wetsuit folliculitis or inflamed hair follicles), make sure that you can get several good flushes before you head in and thoroughly rinse out your wetsuit afterward in fresh water.

Aahhh...

Booties, Hoods, and Gloves

As the water gets cooler, surfers first add neoprene booties, then a neoprene hood, and finally neoprene gloves. Neoprene booties should be tucked underneath your wetsuit leg cuffs to prevent the booties from scooping up water. Some surfers wear booties in warm water to protect their feet from coral reefs and rocks. Booties come in 2 mm neoprene for the tropics, 3 mm for cool water, 5 mm for cold water, and 7 mm for frigid water.

tuck bootie inside wetsuit cuff

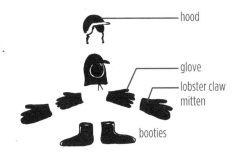

hood

glove

lobster claw mitten

booties

don't forget to apply sunscreen in all exposed places

surf trunks protect legs from wax rash

Booties should fit a bit more snugly than regular shoes but not as tight as climbing shoes to avoid restricting your circulation.

Unlike booties, hoods with collars should not be tucked inside your wetsuit neck collar, to prevent water from flushing inside your wetsuit. Hoods with a visor help keep the sun out of your eyes.

As for gloves, 2, 3, or 5 mm neoprene will help keep the feeling in your fingers. An even warmer option is 5 mm surfing mittens, called lobster claws. Some surfers use webbed gloves for faster paddling.

Other Protective Gear

More and more surfers are wearing protective gear such as ear plugs, sun hats, and surfing goggles. (See page 167.)

Helmets

Formerly helmets were used only when riding powerful waves over shallow reefs, but now surfers are wearing them everywhere to protect themselves from surfboards (their own and others). Gath surfing helmets are lightweight and popular.

Waterproof Sunscreen

Always. Wear. Waterproof. Sunscreen. Ultraviolet (UV) rays can pierce right through overcast skies and reflect off the water to burn you in places you've never been sunburned before. Don't forget the tips of your ears, the gap between your rash guard and your surf trunks, and the backs of your knees.

Surf Trunks

Despite what surfing ads suggest, buying the newest surf trunks will not automatically make your backside off-the-lip maneuvers any better. Although any type of shorts will work, surf trunks should be long enough to protect the inside of your thighs from wax rash while straddling your surfboard and be quick drying to prevent chafing when on land. The front of the trunks should not have any buckles or zippers, which can make lying on your surfboard uncomfortable. Surf trunks should have pockets with drain holes and a cord to loop car keys through. Women should select a one- or two-piece swimsuit that will stay in place after a wipeout; they may also elect to wear surf trunks to avoid wax rash.

Rash Guards

Long- and short-sleeve nylon or polypropylene rash guards and neoprene tops reduce sun exposure in warm waters, ward off windchill, and prevent wax rash. These layers can also be used under a regular wetsuit on particularly chilly days or to help prevent wetsuit rash.

TYPES OF SURFERS

Here is a field guide to the types of surfers you are likely to find sharing the sand and surf with you:

Grommets

Grommets are youngsters who are totally fixated on surfing, not to be confused with beginner surfers. Goofy, gangly, and totally stoked, grommets will swarm out in the lineup after school is over. The best little rippers are often sponsored by a local surf shop. Expect to get showered with spray as they surf past you.

Returning and Seasoned (Vintage) Surfers

Returning surfers are those who surfed in their youth, got distracted by careers or families, and now are returning to the sport 20 years older and 40 pounds heavier. Modern longboards (along with ibuprofen) have helped this older generation of surfers get back in the water again. Seasoned, or vintage, surfers never left the water.

Watermen

These all-around watermen and women live, eat, and breathe anything to do with the water—surfing, bodysurfing, scuba diving, spearfishing, paddleboard paddling, swimming, fishing, outrigger canoeing, and sea kayaking—and excel at all of it. They shape their own boards, winter in Hawaii, and go on exotic boat-based surf expeditions to cool, mysto places with exotic names like "Nias" and "Indo." If they haven't had their photos in the mags, it is only because they didn't want their secret surf spot exposed.

Longboarders

Longboard aficionados are serious surfers who are more into yoga than Xboxes and favor a smooth style over a slash and shred attitude. These folks have tried shortboarding and returned to longboards not for the ease of use but for the aesthetics. For vacations they migrate to classic mellow point breaks in warm climates.

Locals

These are your stereotypical hardcore surfers. They have moved past the grommet stage and are now entirely focused on surfing. Their surf travels lead them to places best described as "sick," "gnarly," "hardcore," or "heavy." Locals openly express disdain for non-local surfers and wish inlanders would stop moving to the coast. A favorite local expression is, "If it's tourist season, why can't we shoot them?"

An interesting variety of the local surfer is surf shop dudes and gals. Surf shop staff know where the party is happening and where the best wave is breaking, but don't expect them to share this information with you. Surf shop owners and surfboard shapers are worth getting to know for expert advice, but customer service can vary tremendously. You may need to understand "dude-speak" to have a meaningful conversation. If you are lucky, they can set you up with good gear, good deals, and good advice. If you are unlucky, you are not even likely to get the time of high tide.

Grommet   Vintage Surfer   Watermen/Women

Hardcore locals are locals who have had enough with tourons and non-local surfers and formed xenophobic tribes to protect their home surf breaks. They are intolerant of kooks, non-locals, and anyone else deemed inferior. Most visual or vocal displays do not result in physical harm, although they will utilize verbal threats and vandalize cars to make their point. Best left well alone. When they travel, they tend to bring their attitude with them.

Kooks

The nerds of the surfing world, kooks are beginner and intermediate surfers in the wrong place or not following proper etiquette. These are clueless surfers who are in over their head or out of place, thus endangering themselves and others. Hopefully reading this book will help you avoid becoming a kook.

Everyday Surfers

These are everyday people who just like to surf. They aren't the best surfers in the water and they aren't the worst. They are dads and moms and granddads and grandmothers with regular jobs. They don't have the time to be in the best of shape, so they often use longboards or funboards, which make everything a little bit easier.

Beginners

Wonderfully naïve, beginners need to find appropriate places and conditions to surf to avoid becoming kooks. Ideally beginners buy this book, attend a surf school, and have buddies who surf who can show them the ropes. For surf vacations, beginners should select beginner-friendly breaks with a surf school. Beginners should keep in mind that other beginners are actually quite dangerous, and all of them should give one another plenty of space.

Longboarder

Local (also see surf shop dude and hardcore local)

Kook

Everyday Surfer

The Coast:
A Beginning Surfer's Guide to Da Beach

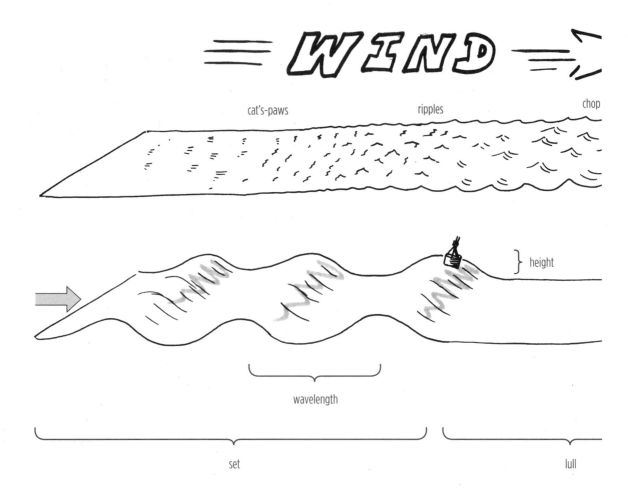

Waves absorb the wind energy of huge storms spanning hundreds of miles, transmit the energy as swells, and then release a concentrated version of the storm's energy in the surf zone. Think of the surf zone as a hundred-mile-wide storm condensed into a few hundred feet.

Although the terms **wave** and **swell** are sometimes used interchangeably, most often a wave refers to an individual wave at the beach ("I had a great ride on that last wave!"), and a swell refers to an unbroken wave in open water ("We're not going to catch any waves way out here in these swells"). More commonly, the term swell is used to describe an entire series of waves associated with a particular storm ("The swell from Hurricane Hugo was epic"). A **set** refers to a cluster of waves arriving in a group, and a **lull** is a calm gap between sets. The term **seas** refers to the general state of the ocean (calm, confused, rough, building, fully developed).

"The waves, unashamed,
In difference sweet,
Play glad with the breezes,
Old playfellows meet."

—Ralph Waldo Emerson, *The Sphinx*

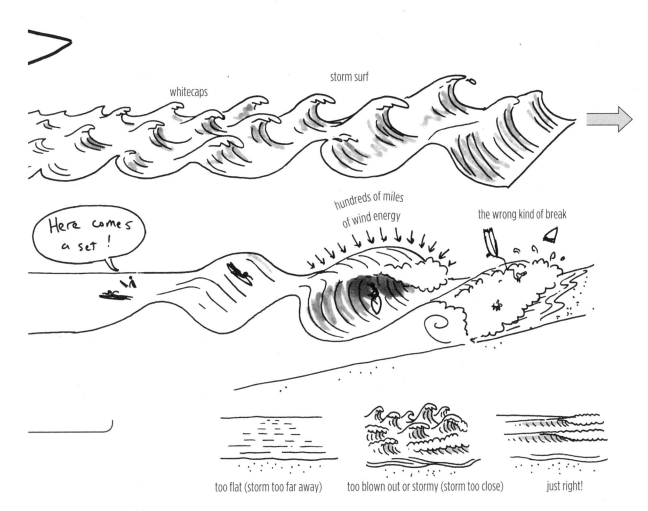

too flat (storm too far away)   too blown out or stormy (storm too close)   just right!

Unlike most other sports, you can't go surfing whenever you want to. At any given surf spot, there may be rideable waves only 50 percent of the time. Surfable waves are entirely dependent on winds and storms someplace out at sea combined with favorable conditions on the coast, all of which vary from place to place and hour to hour. Most of the time the surf may be too flat or too stormy to surf. The sporadic occurrence of high-quality waves is why surfers drop everything when the surf is up, simply because the waves may not be there the next hour, day, week, or month.

To maximize your chances of scoring some waves, you need a basic understanding of the weather that makes surf (meteorology), how waves travel (oceanography), and how waves break (coastal geomorphology).

THE LIFE CYCLE OF A SWELL

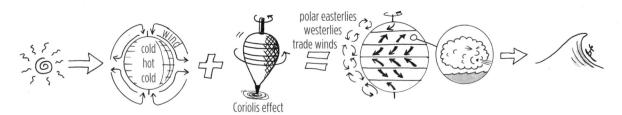

Coriolis effect

polar easterlies
westerlies
trade winds

Weather or Not . . .

As you learned in seventh grade, sunshine warms the air at the equator more than at the poles. Hot air expands and rises, forming an area of low pressure in the tropics that sucks surface air in. Cold air sinks at the poles, forming an area of high pressure that pushes surface air outward. Wind is simply air moving from high- to low-pressure areas. Add a little Coriolis spin from the Earth's rotation, and some additional air cells, and you have the major wind patterns.

When warm air masses mix it up with cold air masses, a localized vortex can form where winds spiral around the storm center. A weather map of such a storm would look like a topographical map of Mount Everest, with the pressure lines, or isobars, close together, indicating a large pressure gradient and strong winds. When the wind whips across oceans, downwind surfers get excited.

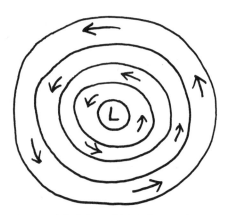

wind spirals counterclockwise around
a northern hemisphere low-pressure system
(clockwise in southern hemisphere)

The Wind-Wave Connection

Making waves is messy. It involves a lot of wind, whitecaps, froth, foam, and spray. The stronger the wind (50 miles per hour vs. 15 mph), the longer it blows (5 days vs. 5 hours), and the greater the fetch, or distance, over which the wind blows (500 miles vs. 50 miles), the bigger the seas. Without wind there would be no waves (except for seismic sea waves, or tsunamis), so surf forecasters look for storms and low-pressure systems.

The friction of the wind across the water's surface agitates molecules into little circular motions. Even though the molecules return to their original position, they pass this energy downwind, where it builds into fan-shaped ripples or cat's-paws, ripples, and chop. All these small waves meld together into bigger and bigger waves as long as the wind keeps blowing. If the waves are big enough, they disperse beyond the stormy area and sort themselves into silent swells.

Center of the Storm

Just as trying to snowboard in a whiteout blizzard is challenging, the conditions for making waves are usually not good conditions for surfing them. Tropical storms, typhoons, and hurricanes are perfect wave nurseries, but not the places you want to hang out on your vacation. The closer the storm to shore, the more mixed up and chaotic the waves. Although a storm can act like a pebble dropped in a pond and radiate waves in all directions, if the storm itself is moving, the wind and waves will be stronger in the direction of that movement.

waves radiate away from storms, particularly in the direction the storm is moving

Surfing in the middle of a storm is not recommended. Waves of all sizes are violently stacked on top of one another, and there are no lulls between sets that allow a surfer to paddle out easily. Ideally a storm will be generating waves far enough from you so that all the waves have organized themselves into sets of waves separated by lulls, and you can enjoy clean swells, blue skies, and favorable winds.

Maps and models showing current and projected winds will give you an idea of whether or not you will be in the center of the storm.

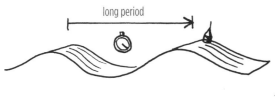

long period

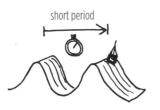

short period

Wave Spacing: Wavelength and Period

Although surfing newcomers focus first on **swell height** (the height of unbroken waves in open water), experienced surfers are more interested in the spacing between waves. The spacing can be measured by the distance between wave crests (**wavelength**) or, more commonly, by the time (**period**) it takes for subsequent wave crests to pass by a fixed point, such as an anchored boat. **Wind chop** has a period of 3 to 8 seconds, **wind swells** have a period from 9 to 12 seconds, and **ground swells** have a period of 13 seconds or more (for a detailed explanation, check out http://www.stormsurf.com/).

long period waves with large wavelengths are faster
than short period waves with short wavelengths

1 car every 20 seconds

long period ground swell

1 car every 3 seconds

short period wind swell

In general, the longer the wave period and wavelength, the higher the wave quality. Long period swells are faster, more powerful, deeper, and travel farther than short period swells of the same height. Long period swells (with one wave passing by every 20 seconds) may seem slower than short period swells (with one wave passing by every 3 seconds), but long period waves have much greater space between wave crests. More short period waves may pass by in a given time period, but that is simply because the waves are close together to begin with, not because they are faster. As an analogy, consider how cars that are farther apart (with a greater wavelength) travel much faster than a traffic jam (short wavelength) of cars that are bumper to bumper. Which would you rather be riding?

Out of the wave mosh pit at the center of a storm, waves of all sizes are flung outward. The longer a storm lasts, the more choppy, short period waves meld together into more surfable long period waves. The fastest swells with the longest periods quickly race in front of the others, forming a swell front and leaving the pokey, disorganized storm chop far behind. These swells can travel for

swells are great travelers

thousands of miles—even across the Pacific from Antarctica to Alaska.

Maps and models of swell periods show well-organized platoons of long period waves marching away from the storm center, followed by the next longest waves, and finally by the slow, short period wind chop that signals the end of a swell. The long period waves often overtake short period waves left over from previous weather systems and are visible on swell models as a wave front.

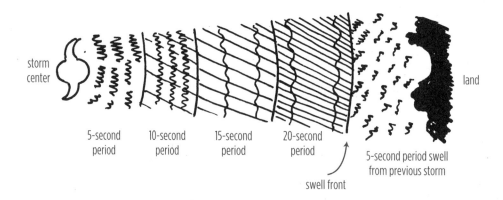

storm center | 5-second period | 10-second period | 15-second period | 20-second period | swell front | 5-second period swell from previous storm | land

Wave Height (in Open Water)

Wave height in open water is a helpful measure of the intensity of a storm (wind strength, duration, and distance), but it needs to be viewed in context.

First, big waves don't necessarily mean good surf, particularly at this stage in your career. Second, the highest waves are in the center of the storm where the winds are strongest, but the waves here are generally far too chaotic and jumbled for surfing. As swells travel outward from the storm's center, the wave height decreases, but the storm's energy has hopefully been captured in any long period swells racing ahead. Wise surfers travel to where these lower-height, longer-period waves are heading and leave the hectic storm surf alone.

Third, wave height as measured by open-water buoys may not correlate well with wave height at your home break. Depending on the swell period, swell direction, and bottom topography, a 5-foot open-water swell that hits your beach could crest as 10-foot breakers or shrivel into ripples.

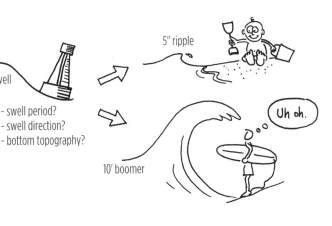

5' swell
- swell period?
- swell direction?
- bottom topography?

5" ripple

Uh oh.

10' boomer

How Waves Travel

Just as you learned from that silly seventh-grade science experiment with a stretched-out slinky, waves move through a medium with a little jiggle but leave the particles in their original position. In the case of ocean waves, individual water molecules, as well as gulls and surfers, do a circular shimmy as the wave energy passes through them. In addition to moving up and down, waves also move you seaward (out) and then shoreward (in). In spite of this surging motion, surfers rarely get seasick. (If you start feeling a little woozy, keep an eye on the horizon to ward off seasickness.)

Waves lose energy, or decay, over time, particularly when opposing winds hit them. Because shorter period waves have shorter wavelengths, they have steeper faces, which catch opposing surface winds that whittle them down in size. Longer period swells or ground swells extend deeper underwater and have less wind resistance, making them able to travel farther than shorter period swells. The upshot is that offshore winds can help "clean up" a swell by eliminating any messy wind chop and leaving the ground swell.

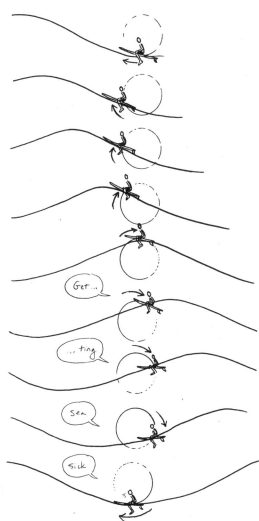

Get...

...ting

sea

sick

short period waves don't last long in opposing winds

Swell Direction

Just because a storm is out there somewhere doesn't guarantee good waves. For wind to send waves your way, it has to be blowing in the right direction. I've been at the beach and watched waves start there and blow out to sea toward some surfer in Iceland. In addition, surf breaks can be shielded from certain swells by offshore islands and reefs, so the swell direction and exposure of the coast can have a big effect on wave action.

An incoming swell hitting a beach straight on may create huge surf, while a neighboring beach facing in a different direction might experience only a glancing blow and the surf there will be flat. Swell angles are usually measured in compass degrees (270 degrees) or cardinal directions (east or west, et cetera). As with wind, the description denotes which quadrant a swell is coming from. For example, a north wind and a north swell come *from* the north. Directions for currents, by contrast, flow toward the direction given, with a south current flowing *to* the south.

Maps and models of swells have arrows depicting the swell direction.

Swell Trend

As you are assessing when and where to go out, it is important to know what a storm is doing and if the swell is rising or fading. In some places, such as Hawaii, the swell can rise extremely quickly, and you might be caught by a rising swell and find yourself over your head (literally and figuratively) in less than an hour.

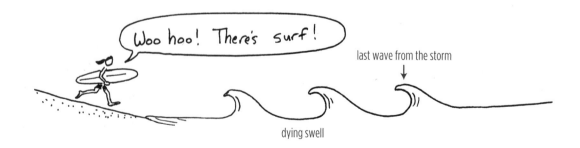

Refraction Action

Just like an iceberg, most of a wave extends underwater. And just as the twin hulls of a well-built catamaran bind the boat together, the wide edges of a well-organized wave travel together as a unified wave front. Think of a catamaran or wave approaching the shoreline at an angle. When the daggerboard or keel of the catamaran hull closest to the shore hits and drags on the bottom, the boat pivots toward shore. In the same way, if one edge of a wave front hits shallow water first, the whole wave bends, or refracts, in that direction. This is how waves wrap around coastlines and islands.

The longer the period and the deeper the wave extends underwater, the sooner the bottom of the wave starts dragging and the easier it is for a wave front to wrap around the shoreline. Only larger period swells wrap around obstacles such as islands or points and reach otherwise protected beaches. These are called ground swells because their deep roots "feel" the ground far out at sea, in contrast to shallow-rooted wind swells.

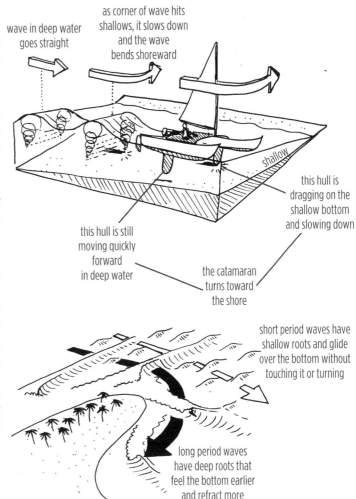

wave in deep water goes straight

as corner of wave hits shallows, it slows down and the wave bends shoreward

shallow

this hull is dragging on the shallow bottom and slowing down

this hull is still moving quickly forward in deep water

the catamaran turns toward the shore

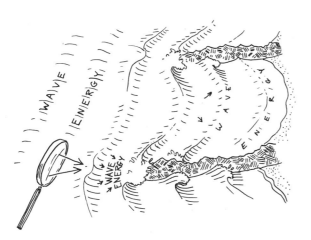

short period waves have shallow roots and glide over the bottom without touching it or turning

long period waves have deep roots that feel the bottom earlier and refract more

WAVE ENERGY

WAVE ENERGY

By bending the wave front, the ocean bottom can either concentrate or dissipate wave energy. Just as a magnifying glass can focus light rays, a headland or reef can amplify wave energy in a central location. These locations are known as **swell magnets** because the surf tends to be larger here than anywhere else. By the same principle, a bay can dissipate wave energy by spreading it out over a wide beach.

Surf Forecasts

Surf conditions often correspond to global wind patterns and seasonal storm cycles, enabling surfers to make an informed guess as to when there might be waves. Winter storms off Alaska produce the famous waves on the north shores of the Hawaiian Islands, while winter storms in the South Pacific send waves up to the south shores of Hawaii six months later. Fall hurricanes off the East Coast of the United States can generate excellent waves. Knowing the general patterns before you go out maximizes your chance of finding surf that fits your abilities.

Regarding the current surf conditions, in the old times you had to actually drive to the beach and check the waves yourself, or call a surf shop for a surf report of questionable reliability. Modern high-tech surf reports and forecasting techniques use geosynchronous satellites, spectral density buoy reports, and advanced modeling with swell decay tables. Today's wave models look more like CAT scans than surfing reports and are filled with similar amounts of information. Surf forecasts show present conditions and use models to project conditions 12, 24, and 72 hours or more into the future. Web camera footage is also available via computer and cell phone to show you the current conditions in real time. Surfline.com and stormsurf.com are two popular surf report websites.

Surf forecasts can contain an overwhelming amount of information. A typical forecast might read, "A 12-foot swell with a period of 15 seconds is expected to arrive at Surfer's Beach at 9:30 a.m. today coming from the northwest at 330 degrees on top of a secondary 2-foot wind swell with a period of 3 seconds coming from the southwest at 225 degrees. Surface winds are expected to be calm in the morning, then rise to 15 to 20 knots from the southwest in the afternoon. . . ."

To translate this information overload into something comprehensible, focus on the following factors: surface winds, sea height, swell direction, and swell period.

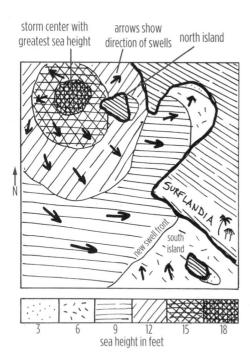

Sea height and swell direction. The oncoming storm pushed by prevailing winds is generating a 12-foot west swell. The brunt of the swell is hitting the north island head, but the swell hasn't reached the south island yet.

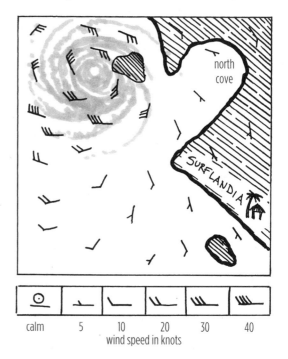

Surface winds. Wind maps use arrows to show wind direction. The more "feathers" on the arrow, the stronger the winds. This example shows a strong storm just off the coast, but winds nearshore are still light.

Swell period. The buoy reports and models show choppy conditions with 5-second periods in the center of the storm, a wind swell of 10 seconds around the perimeter, and ground swells of 15 seconds the farthest out. Although the north island has the biggest waves, the wind and swell period models show that the storm is blown out and disorganized.

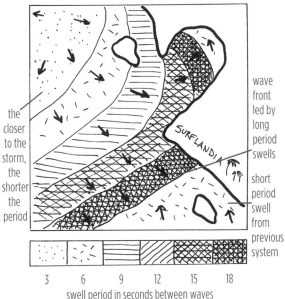

the closer to the storm, the shorter the period

wave front led by long period swells

short period swell from previous system

swell period in seconds between waves

3 6 9 12 15 18

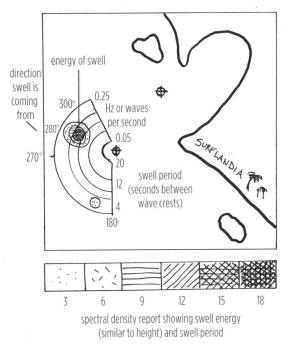

direction swell is coming from

energy of swell

0.25 Hz or waves per second

0.05

swell period (seconds between wave crests)

spectral density report showing swell energy (similar to height) and swell period

3 6 9 12 15 18

A **spectral density** (left) report is a graphic depiction of the swell energy (similar to wave height), period (the longer the better), and direction (hopefully heading your way). In this example, a buoy shows a high-energy swell coming from 280 degrees at a period of 15 seconds and a low-energy wind swell from 185 degrees with a period of 5 seconds.

If you're looking for monster surf, head for Surflandia Point, where the swell is being focused on the headland. There will also be excellent waves peeling down the point. If you are a mere mortal, there should be more manageable waves wrapping into the north cove. The winds are cross-shore but will switch onshore and increase significantly in the afternoon, so an early start is recommended. None of the other breaks are surfable with this swell. Ideally, the storm will sit offshore and spin in place, generating more waves. If the storm moves closer to shore, conditions will deteriorate and folks should stay out of the water.

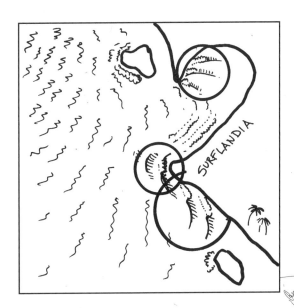

TIDES

tide too high . . .

Because tides affect the depth of the water, they are crucial in determining how, when, and where waves break (and how deep the water is when you wipe out). Some surf breaks are relatively unaffected by the tide, while others are totally tide dependent.

tide too low . . .

If the tide is too high, waves may be **mushy** (see page 73) or not break at all. If the tide is too low, rocks and reefs may be too shallow or waves may break all at once.

Tides can also affect access to the surf. Low tide might mean a dicey walk across a sharp reef, while high tide might mean a difficult exit if waves are slamming against the cliff.

Surf shops, surf schools, and kindly locals can tell you what the particular tidal needs are for local surf breaks. Because the tide changes throughout the day, take note if the reef or sandbar you are surfing over is chest deep or ankle deep.

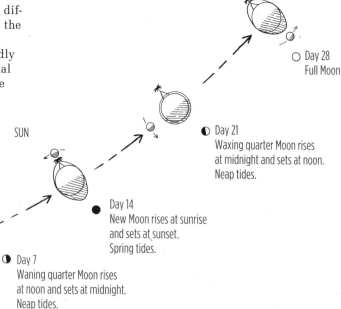

Ups and Downs (Tide Mechanics)

The Earth, Moon, and Sun are in a three-way tug of war with one another for the Earth's oceans. The Moon's gravity creates high tides in the oceans closest to the Moon, while centrifugal force forms high tides in the oceans farthest from the Moon (the Earth and the Moon spin around each other like square-dancing partners). Low tides form between these bulges, where the water is drawn away.

When the Moon is not directly above the equator, it pulls water unequally from the northern and southern hemispheres, creating subsequent high and low tides of different heights.

The Sun can either enhance or diminish the Moon's influence, depending on where the Moon is in its 28-day orbit around the Earth (evident by the phase of the Moon). High-amplitude, or spring, tides result every two weeks when the Moon and Sun line up during a full or new moon. When the Moon and Sun are at a 90-degree angle during the intervening weeks, their gravitational forces are at odds with each other and result in minimal tidal ranges, or neap tides.

Tide Timing

The daily timing of the tides is specific to the location on the coast. In some places there can be two high tides and two low tides every day (with 6 hours between high tide and low tide); in other places there can be just one high tide and one low tide every day (with 12 hours between high tide and low tide). Because the Moon rises 50 minutes later each day, the tides occur roughly 50 minutes later each day.

Tide ranges vary from a few inches to a towering 40 feet. Tides are measured from the mean lower low-water level (just think fairly low water), which means that negative, or minus, tides (0.0 feet or lower) may happen only a few times a month and are noteworthy.

Most surf shops have free, pocket-size tide charts by the front counter. You can also check the tides in the newspapers, on the weather channel, and of course the Internet. If you leave your tide table on your kitchen table, you can determine the tide from any critters and debris that are exposed, and then extrapolate the next high and low tide.

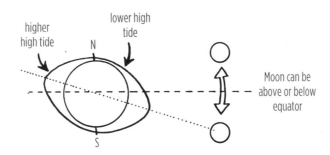

THE SURF ZONE

As waves enter shallow water, the lower part of the wave drags along the bottom, while the wave crest speeds ahead. The bottom eventually trips up the wave crest, sending the top of the wave crashing ahead, or breaking, in a pile of whitewater. The area between where the wave first breaks and where it washes up on shore is the **surf zone**. The frothy bits of the broken wave are known as the soup or whitewater.

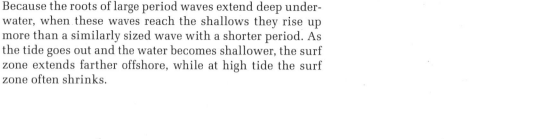

A wave of a certain height breaks when the water is about one and a half times as deep as the height of the wave. The bigger the waves, the farther out they break and the bigger the surf zone. Because the roots of large period waves extend deep underwater, when these waves reach the shallows they rise up more than a similarly sized wave with a shorter period. As the tide goes out and the water becomes shallower, the surf zone extends farther offshore, while at high tide the surf zone often shrinks.

Surf Zone Anatomy and Wave Features

The **impact zone** is where the waves break most frequently. Objects farther from shore are referred to as being **outside**; objects closer to the beach are **inside**. For example, if a large set looks as though it will break farther outside than the pack of waiting surfers, the first surfer to notice it will often warn, "Outside!" Beginning surfers should learn to stand up by staying "inside" and catching the whitewater from previously broken waves. The surf zone may also contain deep troughs or channels where the waves do not break.

Understanding the features of a breaking wave will help you learn which waves to look for and which waves to look out for. Then you will be able to accurately describe the epic wipeout you had when you were "in the green room at a mysto point break but were crushed by the lip."

Types of Waves

A wave can break in three basic ways and in an infinite number of variations. Just like a mountain biker hitting a bump and crashing, waves cruise blissfully through the ocean until they hit shallow water, where they wipe out and break.

The shape and depth of the bottom determines the type of wipeout. The severity of the crash changes with the size of the wave (height and period), the depth of the bottom (tide), and the surface winds. Waves may break one way on the outside, and then re-form and break differently on the inside.

wave hurtling toward shore

? unknown bottom shape

crest pitches over, forming a tube

steep rise = plunging wave (offshore winds and low tides help)

Plunging (Hawaii Five-O) waves. A plunging wave abruptly hits a steep, shallow reef or beach and does a classic end-over-end wipeout. As its crest pitches out over the rest of the wave, it forms a **barrel** (also known as the **tube**, or **green room**). The **peak** is the section where the wave crest or **lip** first starts curling overhead. Often featured in magazines and movies, these dramatic waves are incredibly powerful, and surfing them requires a great deal of experience. Offshore winds can help create plunging waves by delaying the crest from falling. In the beginning of your surfing career, avoid these waves. Steer clear of any places where these waves break directly onto rocks or a beach.

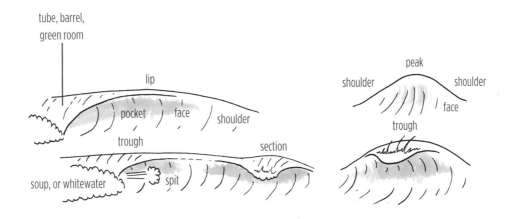

tube, barrel, green room · lip · pocket · face · shoulder · trough · section · soup, or whitewater · spit · peak · shoulder · shoulder · face · trough

gently sloping bottom = spilling wave
(high tides and onshore winds help)

Spilling waves. Like a wobbly mountain biker dabbing left, then right, and losing a water bottle before finally sliding out, a spilling wave loses its energy gradually. The wave crest stumbles over a gently sloping bottom and gradually crumbles into foam without forming a hollow tube. This is the best type of wave for beginning surfers. (But because of the shallow beach profile needed to form these waves, the surf zone often extends far offshore, and it may be a long paddle outside.) Onshore surface winds can help collapse the wave crests to form spilling waves.

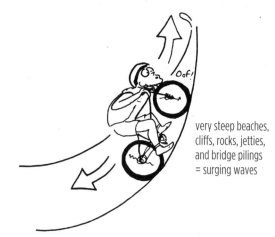

very steep beaches, cliffs, rocks, jetties, and bridge pilings = surging waves

Surging waves. To simulate a surging wave, ride a mountain bike straight up a steep hill or skateboard ramp, stall out, and slide back down without toppling over. With a surging wave, if the bottom is deep enough and the shoreline steep enough, the bottom of the wave can stay under the top and the wave never breaks. Instead, the wave washes up the beach intact, bounces off the steep shoreline, and heads back to sea, disappearing into deeper water. These waves are not surfable (except on a skimboard), and, if you need to, you can paddle your surfboard right next to rocks, pilings, or cliffs without having any whitewater wash you against them. But be aware that bigger waves or a change in the tide (and thus the bottom depth) can cause waves to break instead of surge.

Off steep beaches, the mass of water returning to the sea from a surging wave can form an ocean-going wave also known as **backwash** (see page 62). When the outgoing backwash meets an oncoming wave, unintentionally acrobatic surfing maneuvers are often the result. When you are surfing a wave in and see backwash coming your way, bend your knees or lie down on your board and prepare for some extra bounce. If the backwash is sizable, you may want to kick out or bail before the waves collide.

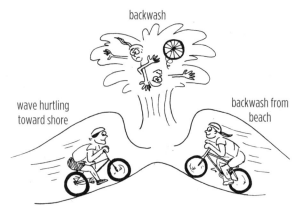

backwash

wave hurtling toward shore

backwash from beach

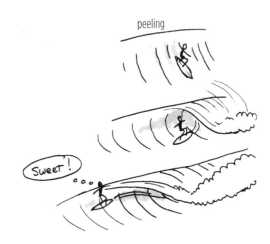

Peeling vs. closing out or dumping. In addition to learning how the wave crest breaks (plunging, spilling, surging), surfers need to know if the wave closes out or peels. **Closeouts** are when the entire wave front crashes or dumps at once, making any ride on the unbroken green face extremely short and generally not worth surfing.

Peeling waves break at one end and gradually feather across the wave front, like a line of falling dominoes providing a continuously moving patch of unbroken wave to surf on. Rides lasting longer than a minute and several hundred yards are possible in peeling surf. A **section** is a length of wave that breaks all at once instead of peeling. Sections usually signal the end of the ride or can be an opportunity for advanced maneuvers around them (more later). Often waves are a combination, peeling in some parts and breaking in sections in others.

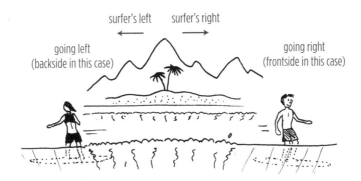

View from the Shore

Breaking left or right. The direction in which a peeling wave breaks is described from the perspective of a person surfing the wave toward shore, similar to skier's left on a ski slope, or river right on a whitewater river. From the shore, going left on a wave looks as though you are going right. Because most surfers stand with the same foot forward while they are surfing, they are either facing the wave (**frontside**) or have their backside to the wave (**backside**). Most surfers are more comfortable surfing a wave in one direction than the other and thus have a preference for surfing waves right or left.

Currents Created by Waves

Wave action can create currents as strong as those in rivers. Before getting in the water, anticipate where the currents might take you and what your escape strategy will be.

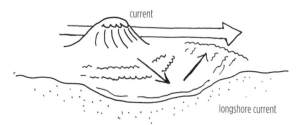

current

longshore current

Longshore, or littoral, currents. Longshore currents flow parallel to the beach and are created when waves approach the beach at an angle and push water in the direction they are breaking. When you are in a longshore current, you may feel that you are not moving because you and the water are moving at the same speed, but a quick look shoreward will show that you are drifting. This current may not be as strong outside the surf zone, or may even be moving in a different direction. Surfers waiting for waves often have to paddle to keep their position. If you don't mind drifting, keep an eye ahead for where you are heading, what types of breaks you are passing through, and what the exit points are like.

Not so fast!

undertow

Undertow and backwash. Undertow is the boogeyman of the beach, representing a blend of fact and superstition somewhere between the Bermuda Triangle and riptides. The concept of an undertow is simple. A wave crest throws a large amount of water up the beach, above the sea level. The undertow is the movement of that mass of water back down into the sea (usually timed to when you are trying to get out of the shore break). Undertow is an intermittent phenomenon. Once the water has drained, the seaward flow stops. The next wave washing up the beach will create another undertow. The undertow effect can be particularly pronounced on steeper beaches.

backwash

This is really important stuff!

LIFE GUARD

The undertow is serious in that it can sweep small children (and not so small adults) off their feet and carry them into deeper water. The person may not have the wherewithal to ride the next oncoming surge back up the beach.

Backwash is a wave bouncing off a steep beach (see Surging Waves, above) and heading back out to sea. When the backwash meets an oncoming wave, the waves momentarily mutate into a double wave, leading to a spectacular wipeout for anyone surfing the wave.

Rip currents. Rip currents (inappropriately called riptides) are narrow streams of water rushing straight out to sea from the beach. Rip currents form when water from breaking waves piles up in a trough between a sandbar and the beach. Where there is a low spot in a sandbar or where the sandbar ends, the excess water pours back out to sea and further erodes this channel. The current then dissipates beyond the surf zone. Flash rip currents are temporary rips created after a particularly large set of waves. Fixed rip currents occur where permanent features such as jetties, breakwaters, rocky points, and piers redirect longshore currents offshore.

If you know what to look for, rip currents can be seen in the surf zone because the wind and waves generate a distinct texture in the outgoing current. Smaller waves may not break in the rip current channel, and there may be a visible cloud of suspended sediment in the outgoing flow.

For surfers, rip currents can serve as a convenient ski lift or conveyer belt back outside for their next wave. For swimmers, rip currents can be deadly. According to the National Oceanographic and Atmospheric Association, more swimmers die in rip currents than from tornadoes, hurricanes, flooding, and lightning combined. Swimming against a rip current is like walking the wrong way on an escalator. If you are caught in a rip current unintentionally, swim perpendicular to the shore and across the channel to the nearest sandbar. From there, swim back to shore, but be aware of longshore currents that may sweep you back into the rip. Another option is to float out with the rip current until it dissipates, then swim parallel to the shore and come in across the sandbar where the waves are breaking.

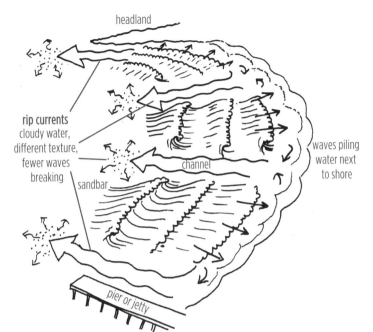

headland

rip currents
cloudy water, different texture, fewer waves breaking

channel

sandbar

waves piling water next to shore

pier or jetty

Much better!

This isn't working!

Time to stop and think.

Oh yeah! I must be in a rip current. I need to paddle parallel to shore!

Types of Surfing Breaks

Although the most obvious features of a wave are its size (always bigger than you think), type (spilling or plunging), and whether it peels left or right or closes out, the type of break is also important. The break refers to the overall environment, the bottom type, and other important features. The type of break determines how you access the waves, how you surf, and what hazards may exist.

Point breaks. Point breaks are where waves peel gradually along a headland and into a bay. In this situation, waves travel more or less along the shoreline instead of directly toward shore, and incredibly long rides are possible. In addition to long rides, point breaks often mean an easy paddle out in the deepwater channel around the surf zone. However, the shoreline and bottom are often rocky, making access to the water tricky. In

addition, the premier breaks have specific takeoff spots, so crowds are common and concentrated.

Reef breaks. Reef breaks are where waves break on a solid bottom such as a coral reef or rock ledge. Underwater features can focus the wave energy and amplify the wave, making the waves here larger than at surrounding breaks. Like point breaks, the bottom topography can allow waves to peel instead of close out, and deepwater channels can allow easy access around the breaking waves. However, the coral or rock bottom can make wipeouts more dangerous, particularly at low tide. The narrow takeoff spot for reef breaks can also be overcrowded.

Beach breaks. Beach breaks are where waves break on an offshore sandbar; they are the most

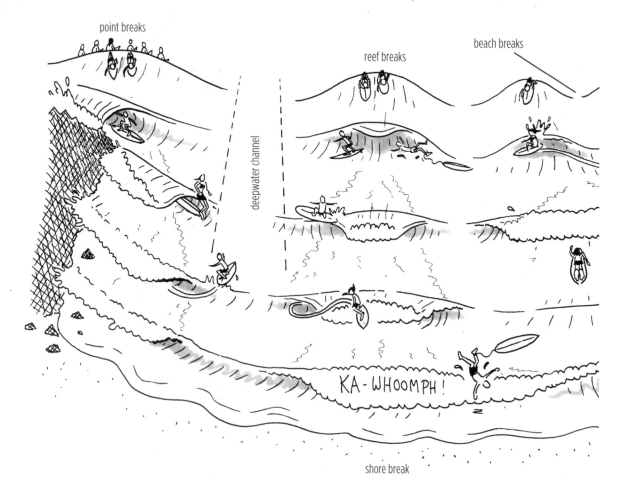

point breaks

deepwater channel

reef breaks

beach breaks

KA-WHOOMPH!

shore break

popular type of break for beginning surfers. To be surfable, a wave has to break far enough offshore to allow room for you to stand up and ride before the wave hits the beach. A wave that simply smacks into the beach is called a shore break (see below). Often there is a trough of deeper water between the offshore sandbar and the shore break. Sandbars can create multiple peaks, which can accommodate more surfers than other breaks. Paddling out through high surf on a beach break can be challenging if there are no channels. Depending on the shape of the incoming waves and the sandbars, waves can either peel (good) or close out (bad). Because sandbars constantly change, surfing conditions at beach breaks can change overnight.

River-mouth breaks. In addition to carrying water to the ocean, rivers also carry massive amounts of sand, gravel, and rocks. The sediment that settles at the river mouth can act like a point break with peeling waves and a deepwater channel for the paddle back out. River mouths can have tricky currents, polluted water, and be sharky, so check with locals about river-mouth breaks before heading out.

Shore breaks. Because shore breaks are where waves slam directly onto the shore, they are not a good place to surf. There isn't enough time or depth to stand up on a wave before breaking your fins (or your back) in the sand. The shore break is the realm of kids boogie boarding and bodysurfing who don't mind rubbing their bellies raw as they ride up onto the beach. All types of breaks can have a shore break between you and the surfable waves offshore. Getting in and out through the shore break can be the hardest part about surfing, so try to minimize your time there.

Jetties, breakwaters, and piers. These man-made sand traps retain sand and build up the beach on one side, while sand erodes from the other side. In addition, a wave can ricochet off these structures and combine with another wave to form a much bigger A-frame wave. The result is often perfectly formed waves for surfers. The rocks, pilings, and rip currents (see page 63) also present significant safety hazards, so surfing here is not recommended for beginners.

jetties, piers, and breakwaters

deepwater channel

river-mouth breaks

WIND EFFECTS ON SURF

While distant winds generate waves, local wind conditions at the beach affect the shape of the waves and the texture of the wave faces, both of which affect the surfability of the waves. For comparison, think of the effects that wind can have on a ski slope. High winds can transform knee-deep powder into an unrideable crust. In the same way, onshore or cross-shore winds can convert otherwise fun waves into unrideable slop.

Strong onshore surface winds or blown-out conditions cause the wave crests to collapse prematurely in deeper water than a wave would normally break in (think of whitecaps on a deep bay), while offshore winds hold the wave crests up longer.

Glassy Conditions

Under calm, windless conditions, the surface of the ocean can take on a smooth, glassy appearance that allows the pure wave shape to manifest itself without interference. Glassy conditions are the equivalent of a bluebird powder day when skiing. The harsh weather conditions that produced the snow, and the surf, have moved on, and the conditions are perfect for being outside and enjoying the effects. Surfing in these conditions is like skating on an ice rink just after the Zamboni machine has groomed it, riding your mountain bike on smooth slickrock sandstone, or skateboarding on freshly cured blacktop. If you have the right combination of swell and bottom shape, glassy conditions can be conducive to tube riding. Offshore kelp beds can reduce the wind chop in incoming waves and help create semi-glassy conditions even in onshore situations.

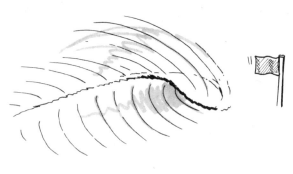

offshore kelp bed

Offshore Winds

Offshore winds hold the wave face up longer, giving surfers more time on the exciting, steepening part of a wave before the crest breaks. Offshore winds can also hollow out the wave like a glassblower shaping molten glass, creating tubes for surfers. In addition, offshore winds are like grooming machines at a ski resort that smooth unrideable bumps into carvable corduroy. If the winds are especially strong, they can have a deleterious effect by creating mini-moguls on the face of a wave and keeping you from catching a wave by blowing against the bottom of your surfboard. Adapt to these conditions by positioning yourself in steeper areas where gravity can assist you and by paddling extra hard when it counts.

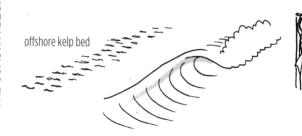

Onshore Winds

Onshore winds generate waves, but they also cause waves to break early by pushing the crest over into the trough prematurely. Waves affected by onshore winds tend to be disorganized, bumpy, choppy,

difficult to predict, and rides tend to be short. Surfing in these conditions is similar to skiing in the rain in tracked-up powder with lots of bumps. If they are not too strong, onshore winds can provide some waves to practice in and no crowds (see Dealing with Imperfect Conditions on page 74).

Cross-Shore Winds

Cross-shore winds overlay a small, short period wind swell at 90 degrees to the main swell. Where the crest of the wind chop intersects the larger unbroken wave, the combined wave is bigger and breaks sooner. Where the trough of the wind chop intersects this wave, the wave breaks later. The end result is that cross-shore winds divide formerly continuous waves into several distinct sections, dramatically shortening the potential length of each ride.

Understanding Wind Patterns

Although surf and weather forecasts can provide useful information on daily winds, it can be helpful to understand wind patterns such as land and sea breezes and seasonal trends.

Land and sea breezes. Land breezes are responsible for motivating otherwise lethargic individuals into waking up at ungodly hours to go surfing. During the day, the sun warms the land surface more quickly than the sea surface. As a result, the air above the land heats up more quickly and rises, creating an area of low pressure. The cool air over the ocean then moves inland to replace it. This is why onshore breezes are common during the day. At night the situation is reversed: the land cools more quickly than the sea, so the air above it cools, sinks, and drains back toward the ocean, forming an offshore wind from evening to early morning. Because of the beneficial effects of calm or offshore winds on wave shape, proficient surfers have learned to schedule their lives around early-morning and late-afternoon surf sessions.

Seasonal patterns. There are seasonal wind patterns as well. Expect easterly trade winds most of the time at places like Bathsheba or Soup Bowls in Barbados and in the Hawaiian Islands. In Costa Rica, summer winds come from the east, creating offshore conditions with some reliability on the west coast. Time your surf vacation to take advantage of these trends. As you are assessing when and where to go out, it is important to know what a storm is doing and whether a swell is rising or fading.

Strong or sustained onshore winds can create unsafe conditions such as large waves, strong longshore currents (see page 62) and riptides, and never-ending sets with no breaks between waves to catch your breath or make it outside.

sea breeze

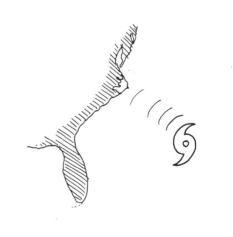

land breeze

PUTTING IT ALL TOGETHER: PICKING A GOOD SPOT TO GO SURFING

A first-time kayaker doesn't put in above a Class IV rapid, and a newbie skier doesn't learn to ski on a black diamond run. As a novice surfer, you should look for the ocean equivalent of the Class I riffle or the bunny slope. Use the following tools to make sure a break is right for you. *When in doubt, don't go out.*

Surfing Guidebooks, Reports, and Forecasts

Books and surf guides have lists of surf spots to consider, but remember that breaks may be surfable less than 50 percent of the time. A highly recommended beginner spot might be totally unsurfable on a particular day due to surf conditions or tide. A fearsome advanced surf spot might be relatively benign on the day you want to go out. Surf reports and forecasts on the Internet can give you an idea of what the conditions for particular breaks but will leave it up to you to figure out what exact spot to go out or if you should go out at all. (By the way, do not leave your surf guidebook on the dash of your rental car, as locals will immediately identify you as an outsider and may give hostile locals yet another reason to harass you.)

Surf Schools

Surf schools know what breaks are most appropriate for that particular time of day (more on surf schools in Chapter 7) and can get you set up with lessons and equipment. Keep in mind that conditions change, and these breaks may not be suitable for your skill level after you have graduated from your surf school.

Surf Shops

The surf shop can also be a useful, if somewhat variable, place to find out basic information about good places to go. Surf shop staff are protective of the better, more advanced surf breaks and will direct you to more mellow places with hordes of other beginners so you won't get in the way of the advanced surfers when they head out after work. Although you won't find directions to the secret spot, you can get tips about the swell and swell forecast, tides for local breaks, places where newcomers are tolerated, and safe places to park your car.

While you're at the surf shop, pick up a local tide table, surf wax, and some stickers to support the local economy.

Lifeguards

Check with the lifeguard at the beach about surf conditions before you go out. Despite their too-cool-to-talk-to TV image, lifeguards love to be asked basic questions (it is better than performing CPR any day), so don't be shy. If it's your first time at this location, just say that you're from out of town and ask if there is anything particular you should be aware of (rocks, reefs, rips, et cetera) and where they would recommend heading out for your particular skill level. Most lifeguards surf (she probably just got out of the water or is planning to go surfing after her shift), so they'll have good recommendations.

Hurry Up and Wait

Once you figure out what breaks might be working, the next thing is to check out the surf yourself. Watch the surf and surfers for ten to twenty minutes while several sets roll through. If you look for only thirty seconds, you might be catching the set of the day or a lull between sets.

If all the surfers are packed in the same place and no one is inside, a wave hasn't come through for a while. If scattered surfers are paddling out through a foamy surf zone, some waves just came through. If the waves are breaking much farther out than the surfers are, this is a large "cleanup set."

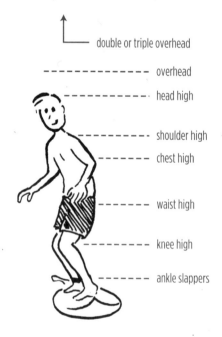

Estimating Wave Height

Few factors are as subjective as the size of a wave. One person's "teensy" may be another person's "ginormous." Some places measure waves from the face as the wave pitches over, while others measure from the back of the wave, which is a much smaller number. Become familiar with the local scale so you know what "6-foot" really means. An 8-foot wave in Florida can mean a 6-foot wave in California and a 4-foot wave in Hawaii.

The least-subjective way to measure waves is relative to the height of a 6-foot-tall surfer. Common terms include ankle slapper, knee high, waist high, chest high, shoulder high, head high, 2 feet overhead, double-overhead, triple overhead, et cetera.

When judging wave height for yourself, remember that the wave is ALWAYS bigger in the water. Use extra caution when checking out the surf from parking lots perched high above the surf. Use binoculars and reference points such as other surfers for scale.

Don't judge a wave just from its size. Depending on how the waves are breaking and what the bottom is made of, smaller waves might be more difficult and dangerous than bigger waves at a different spot.

Judging Wave Height

PARKING LOT PERSPECTIVE	REALITY CHECK
Wow! It's huge!	You won't even make it outside, and if you do, you won't want to be there.
Looks fun!	An epic day. Take extra care to secure your leash.
Huh. Well, it's better than nothing.	Perfect conditions. You'll imagine yourself on the cover of *Surfing Magazine*.
It's soooo flat!	Excellent conditions for your first season of surfing.

Getting In, Out, and Around

Where are surfers getting in and out? How hard is it to get in and out? Where are the waves and currents pushing surfers? Look for exposed and subsurface rocks, pilings, reefs, and debris. Are there any obvious longshore currents or rip currents?

Are surfers continuously battling whitewater to get back outside, or do they have time to paddle out between sets or in an available channel? Gain a sense of how much time you have to paddle out by counting the number of waves in a set and the time between sets. Once outside, are surfers continuously paddling to stay in position while they wait for waves?

Skill Level, Vibe, and Wipeouts

Check out the skill level of the surfers. If the other surfers are consistently getting shot out of the tube, the waves are probably too advanced and you will probably get in the way. Breaks where all the surfers are riding shortboards are often too advanced for beginning surfers.

Also check out the atmosphere in the lineup. Is there a pack of testosterone-charged hotdoggers launching massive aerials or a bunch of mellow old hippies enjoying the day and letting the occasional wave pass unridden? How does your skill level compare? Find a scene that best fits your mood and ability.

How often are other surfers wiping out? How bad are the wipeouts? What happens after they wipe out? Are the waves pushing them into the cliffs or into a sandy beach? If the wipeouts have you saying "ouch" from the beach, imagine what it will be like in the impact zone.

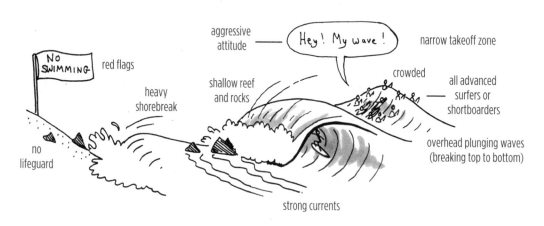

Bad Beginner Break

Asking Other Surfers

Ask other surfers who are leaving what the waves and crowds were like. Because they are finished for the day and don't have to worry about your beginner antics ruining their surf session, they are likely to offer somewhat better advice than other surfers who are about to head out.

Just because the surf is up doesn't mean it's a good place to learn to surf. Steer clear of places where the waves are described as "heavy," "thick," "sick," "gnarly," "pitching," "firing," "pumping," "going off," or "sucking dry." If there are crowds of photographers and spectators at the beach, you may want to find a more protected location. Seek out places where surfers characterize the waves as "mushy," "crumbling," "weak," "gutless," or "mellow." **At this point in your career, mushy is marvelous.**

Warning Signs

Warning signs are posted where folks have gotten into trouble in the past and as a reminder to not be next. Look for any posted warning signs about rip currents, rocks, jellyfish, or water pollution. Was there a recent sewage spill or fish kill? (It happens all too often.) Red flags generally mean that beaches are temporarily closed to swimmers because of dangerous conditions, and the lifeguards are tired of hauling everyone out of the water. Although experienced surfers regularly ignore high surf warnings, you should not.

The storms that bring big surf often overflow local sewage treatment plants and storm drain systems, so raw sewage and other contaminants dump directly into the ocean. Postings about water pollution may be found at the beach as well as in newspapers or on the Internet, but often not immediately (see more on water quality in Chapter 7).

Hard-core surfers often ignore such warning signs and tolerate conditions that would have other communities knocking down the door of the local Environmental Protection Agency office. (It's often considered a badge of courage to put up with unsafe conditions for the sake of good surf.)

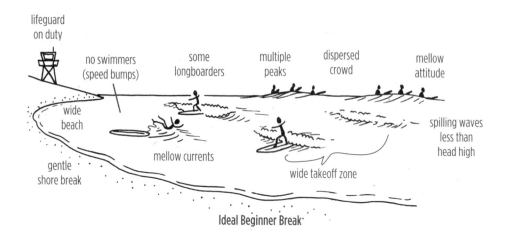

Ideal Beginner Break·

Ideal Beginner Break

The ideal beginner break is a beach break with small, gently spilling waves, multiple peaks, and a lifeguard on duty. Most of the waves are waist high, and the biggest waves are less than head high. The currents are mild, and there are no obstacles (except for other surfers and your own surfboard). Most surfers are riding longboards rather than high-performance shortboards.

The break is distinctly uncrowded and has multiple peaks, which disperse the crowd, as opposed to a point break or a reef break where surfers congregate around a solitary takeoff spot. You will learn faster at a mediocre break with fewer people than at a famous break crowded with lots of people. Be sure to go with a friend; you never want to surf alone, particularly early in your career. *When in doubt, don't go out!*

Dealing with Imperfect Conditions

You don't have to wait for a powder day to learn to snowplow on the bunny slope. At this point in your career, think wave quantity versus quality. The fact of the matter is that substandard waves with imperfect winds occur most of the time. Even in these less-than-ideal conditions, waves may still be surfable and less crowded. Learning in somewhat suboptimal conditions will improve your overall surfing skills so you can take advantage of the good conditions when they happen. Although ideally you will have an empty peak all to yourself, you don't want to be the only person in the water (this tells you that something is way wrong). Even if you are decidedly not picky, never go out when the surf is unsafe.

Never Leave Good Surf

A final word on selecting a break. Once you've found a break that looks good to you and fits all your criteria, you will be tempted to see if the next several spots up the beach are any better. Although there can be some merit in considering all your options, I have seen entire days spent driving around comparing surf spots instead of surfing, only to have the swell die before the end of the day. The bottom line is NEVER LEAVE GOOD SURF! Now that you've found a suitable beginner break, it's time to grab your board.

Getting on the Water

"Haste makes waste."

—Proverb emphasizing patience when waiting for a set to end so you can paddle out

"He who hesitates is lost."

—Proverb emphasizing expedience when you
have a lull between sets to paddle outside

OK. You've checked the current conditions
and the afternoon forecast, talked with the
lifeguard, and scoped out the scene. You know
that the 2- to 4-foot swell with a period of 12
seconds is expected to drop slightly throughout the afternoon. There is a low tide of
1.1 feet at 2:36 p.m., when the rock at the
end of the beach will start sticking out of
the water. The crowd is a mix of beginner and intermediate surfers, with the
more advanced surfers out at the point.

Now (finally!) it's time to get out
of your car and hit the waves! This
chapter tells you everything you
need to know—about getting from
your car, through the waves, and
out to the break.

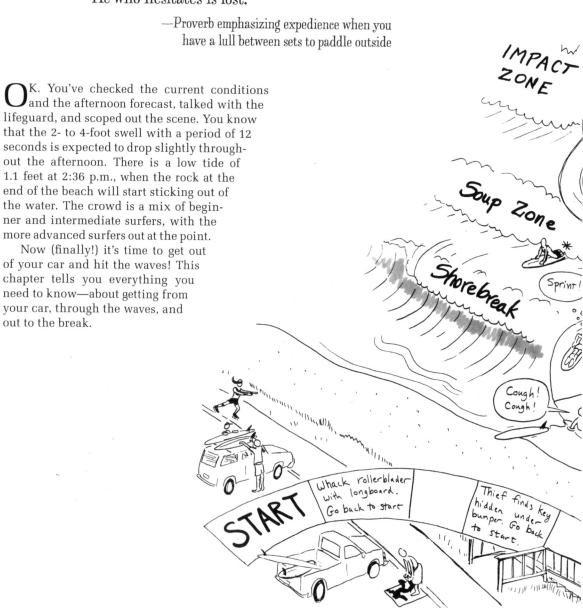

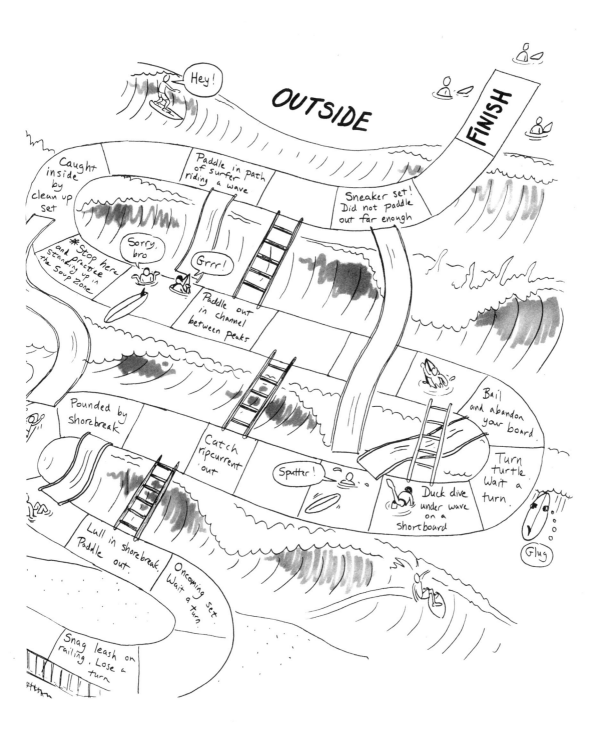

GETTING FROM CAR TO WATER

Hopefully this step will be uneventful, but it helps to avoid parking your car where the ground is covered by shattered safety glass (a sign of past break-ins) or where the car could be ticketed or towed away. Leave valuables at home, or lock them out of sight in the glove compartment or trunk and hope for the best. On windy days, don't leave your surfboard unsecured on the roof of your car. When you take your surfboard off your roof racks, don't set your board behind another car (crunch!) or block the sidewalk.

Changing Clothes

For surfers, the only changing room you need is a beach towel. To prevent random moonings, wrap the towel around your waist, then tuck in a corner and roll it inward or outward. If it's a bit of a walk to the beach, change before starting your hike, or carry your gear in a drip-ready backpack to save your arm strength for the water. If you bring along a beach bag, make sure it doesn't contain anything you don't mind "donating" to a local cause.

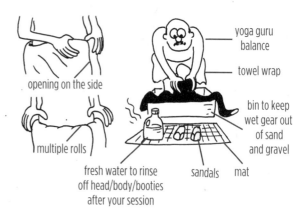

opening on the side

multiple rolls

yoga guru balance

towel wrap

bin to keep wet gear out of sand and gravel

fresh water to rinse off head/body/booties after your session

sandals   mat

A Thieve's Guide to Popular Key-Stashing Spots

with surfer in the water (drat!) ←

wheel well

under a rock on the way to the beach ←

in backpack on beach ←

behind gas cap cover

under bumper

hitch-safe key vault (drat!)

What to Do with Your Car Keys

All good thieves know (or will soon know by watching you) the most common places to hide car keys. The most secure option is to bring your keys with you by securing them in the leash pocket in your surf trunks or wetsuit or in the ankle cuff of your leash. However, all these options are problematic for electronic keys. Some companies now make mini-safes that fit in your tow hitch, among other places, for electronic keys and other valuables. You can also try stashing your key under a recognizable rock on your way to the beach if you are sure that no one is watching you.

Carrying Your Surfboard

There are several ways to carry your surfboard. No matter how you carry it, be mindful of where the fins and ends of the board are. Be aware of bicyclists, joggers, and other folks who do not want to be wiped out by your board, so avoid any Three Stooges moves. Keep your leash wrapped securely around the tail, or hold it coiled in your hand so it doesn't drag or trip you. Because gusts of wind can swing your board around dangerously, you may need to stabilize the board with both hands, or reduce the wind resistance by carrying it right side up against your hip or on your head.

Watch out for pedestrians and bikers!

First, if your board is skinny enough and your arms are long enough, carry the board on edge under your arm. Most surfers carry their board nose first with the fin facing in.

a keen awareness of where the nose, tail, and fins are

leash wrapped securely around tail or held in hands (and not dragging on the ground)

extra hand for wind gusts

long arms help

If you have trouble reaching your arm around your board, carry it fin out so the flat deck is against your body and the curved bottom fits under your arm better.

You can also balance the board on your head, either upside down or right side up. Consider using a towel for padding and to keep the wax out of your hair.

For particularly unwieldy boards, cradle the board in the crook of your arm and rest it against your head and shoulder.

You and your surf buddy can also do a double carry, with one person carrying the noses and the other the tails.

Another option is to make or buy a sling that cradles your surfboard.

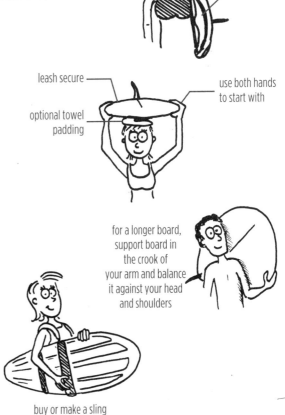

board turned fin out for shorter arms

leash secure

optional towel padding

use both hands to start with

for a longer board, support board in the crook of your arm and balance it against your head and shoulders

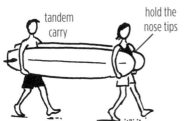

tandem carry

hold the nose tips

buy or make a sling

Stretching

It is always a good idea to spend a few minutes stretching before hitting the waves (and being hit by the waves) and again after your surf session. Yoga is an excellent complement to many sports, including surfing. A good reference for stretching and warming up is *Fit to Surf*, by Rocky Snyder.

Below are some common stretches, but incorporate whatever works best for you. The checkmark shows places on your body where you should be feeling each stretch. Take the time you use to stretch to watch the wave and water conditions.

✔ = places where you should feel something good happening

opposite arm and leg

Highly recommended!

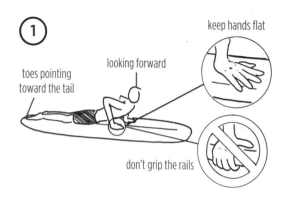

(1)

keep hands flat

toes pointing
toward the tail

looking forward

don't grip the rails

(2)

cobra arch in back

look left, right, and ahead
to make sure the coast is clear

Regular foot!

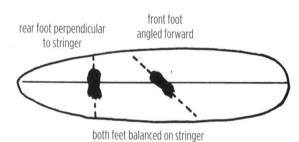

rear foot perpendicular
to stringer

front foot
angled forward

both feet balanced on stringer

Practice Popping Up

Before you get in the water, you need to practice popping up. **Popping up** is the seemingly simple but remarkably challenging act of quickly rising from a prone position on your belly to an athletic position standing on your feet. Making this motion fluid, seamless, and fast is the key to surfing.

Surfers stand on their boards with one foot ahead of the other. Both feet are centered on the **stringer**, or centerline, of the board, with the front foot angled forward at about 45 degrees and the rear foot more perpendicular to the stringer. The **ankle leash** securing your board to you wraps around your rear ankle.

Plan A

push torso up . . .

(3)

. . . and slide both feet underneath you

Which foot is forward is a matter of preference. **Regular footers** have their left foot forward while **goofy footers** have their right foot forward. There is no inherent advantage to either stance. Generally, it is easier to surf across a wave when you are facing it, so regular footers favor waves breaking to the right (**rights**) while goofy footers prefer **lefts**.

If you snowboard, skateboard, windsurf, or wakeboard, use the same stance. If you telemark ski, select which foot you have in front when making your best turns. When dismounting a bike and coasting to the bike rack, see which foot you like having forward. If you are still not sure if you are regular or goofy foot, slide across the kitchen floor with socks on and see which foot you put out in front.

To practice popping up on the beach, scoot the fins into the sand so the tail of the board is supported by the sand and the fins won't break. (1) Lie on the board and place both hands flat on the deck on either side of your chest, closer together than you would for a normal pushup. If you have flexibility issues, you can prop your hands up with your thumb and fingers to be slightly higher off the deck and have more room for your feet. (2) Arch your back to create a space for your legs. (3) Push your torso up with your hands and slide both feet underneath you, keeping your hips close to the board. As you pop up, twist your shoulders in the direction you will be facing. Simultaneously slide both feet under your torso, with your front foot sliding between your hands and your rear foot sliding underneath your butt. Keep your stance wide and low for stability.

If you are having problems popping up in one motion, another option is to first slide your rear foot in place (a), then pop up and scoot your front foot into place (b). Keep in mind that you will eventually have to learn to pop up in one step.

④ Keep looking forward to keep your butt low and your weight low and centered. ⑤ As they say in Ed Guzman's Surf Camps, "Stand tall and fall, or stay low and go."

You can also do this in the comfort of your own living room, using the rug as your surfboard. The better you get at this on dry land, the more time you will spend standing up and surfing and the less time imitating a stiff-limbed zombie going over Niagara Falls.

Plan B: Two-step technique if landing gear is jammed

a — scoot your rear foot into place

b — stand on rear foot and scoot front foot under chest

4 — look ahead / keep butt low

looking down keeps your butt up and makes it hard to balance

5 — bend knees to keep weight low and centered

CHOOSING A LAUNCHING SPOT

Experienced surfers often take sketchy shortcuts to get to the breaking waves. This may mean scaling fences; scrambling up and down cliffs; hurling themselves off rocks, piers, and jetties; and sprinting out between cliff-smashing waves. Before you act like a lemming and follow a bunch of shortboarders jumping off a cliff, make sure you have the water skills, equipment, and sense of timing to deal with these situations. Watch how other surfers get in (and out!) before you try it yourself. Getting in and out is often trickier than it looks.

It is often better to enter at a protected beach and have a longer paddle to the break than to take a dangerous shortcut. From the beach, look for a deep channel with fewer or no waves breaking so you can paddle around the whitewater (and any oncoming surfers). See if you can also get back out the same way you got in, but have a backup exit planned.

If you need to stash any stuff, take note of the last high-tide line (the surf may come up above it). Be wary of stashing stuff and hanging out at the base of unstable cliffs, particularly after a rainstorm.

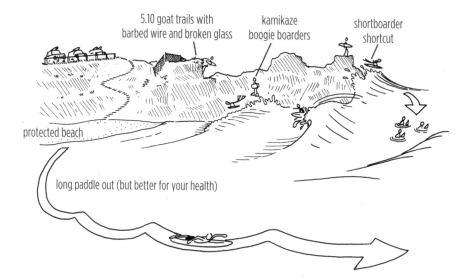

5.10 goat trails with barbed wire and broken glass

kamikaze boogie boarders

shortboarder shortcut

protected beach

long paddle out (but better for your health)

Timing for Entering the Water

The shore break is the first major obstacle you will encounter. If your timing is right, you won't have any problems. If your timing is bad, your surf session might end right there. This is where all the time you spent watching the waves and sets pays off. Try to time your entry during a lull between sets. A few seconds of delay may mean missing your window, so be ready to go. If you miss your chance, it is usually better to wait a few more minutes onshore than to fight your way out through a set. It pays to be patient.

Never Put the Surfboard between Yourself and a Wave

Never hold up the surfboard between yourself and a breaking wave. According to Matt George's *Dictionary of Surfing*, your own surfboard is arguably the most hazardous thing in the water, accounting for more than 50 percent of surfing injuries.

Entering from the Beach

When entering the water from the beach onto a sandbar or shallow reef, carry your surfboard until you can float it beside you at your waist. You never want your fin to drag on the bottom.

When wading out on a sandy bottom, shuffle your feet to shoo off any stingrays and push your surfboard alongside you with one hand. If the sandy bottom is irregular, place both hands on your board for balance while you find your footing.

If the bottom is a reef that is too sharp to walk on and too shallow to paddle over, you can turn your board upside down (frontward or backward) and carefully paddle it through the flatwater with the fin up.

Ideally, you have timed your entrance between waves. If a small wave comes and you are still in shallow water, either push your surfboard through the wave with your hand or lift your surfboard up to your waist and over the wave. If the wave is much taller than your waist and the water is too shallow to turn turtle in (see page 92), you are probably in the wrong spot or at the wrong time. Retreat and reassess.

Once the water is more than waist deep, it is almost always more efficient to start paddling than to keep wading. Most beginners keep walking when they should be paddling and spend more time bouncing up and down on their toes than moving forward. Resist this urge and start paddling as soon as you can.

surfboard to side

shuffle your feet in the sand to shoo off stingrays

stinky feet!

turn your board upside down to paddle across sharp shallow reefs

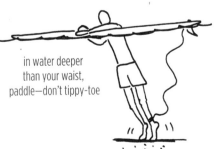

in water deeper than your waist, paddle—don't tippy-toe

Entering from Rocks

Launching from rocks or cliffs is generally not recommended. Waves breaking on rocky shores often have not had a chance to disperse their energy and can be unexpectedly powerful. Every year unsuspecting beachgoers are swept off rocks, cliffs, and jetties by set waves. An easily accessible sandy beach can turn into a minefield of boulders as the tide changes.

· If there are no other alternatives and the surf conditions are mild, entering from a rocky shoreline might be an option after you've gained some experience. Don't forget you also need to be able to get back out of the water. First watch to see how other surfers negotiate the entry and exit and ask them for pointers. Watch how high up the shore the largest waves crash so you know where the safety zones are.

Choose a launch time when no waves are coming so you have time to paddle through the surf zone. Be careful of shallow rocks hidden by the waves. Look for deeper channels between rocks to paddle out through.

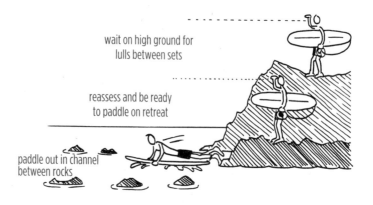

wait on high ground for lulls between sets

reassess and be ready to paddle on retreat

paddle out in channel between rocks

or, on the backside of small waves

If the shore is shallow and rocky, you may want to launch immediately after a small wave surges and covers up the rocks. Launch yourself with a small horizontal leap for momentum and use your arms as shock absorbers. Make sure you have enough time to paddle to deep water before the wave washes back out again or the next wave comes in. This is not a place to linger.

If you are entering deep water from any height, hold your board to the side so you won't land on it, then jump in feet first (never dive). To make sure a loose leash does not become tangled and trap you in the rocks (always bad), take up the slack with your hand, or keep your leash off and coiled in your hand until you are in the water.

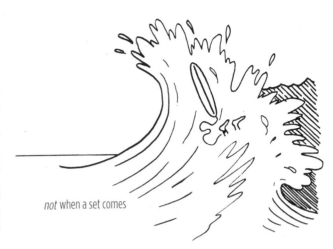

not when a set comes

try not to snag your leash

This is going to be good.

Entering from a Boat

Some surf schools and surf camps offer boat tours, where you are driven along the coast to a surf spot and dropped off from a boat. The great thing about entering the water from a boat is that you don't have to worry about paddling through the shore break and breaking waves to get to the surf, at least not to start with (for more details, see page 163 in Chapter 7).

Before launching from a boat, always coordinate with the boat captain. To avoid tangles, keep mind of your leash as you jump, or keep it wrapped around your board until you are in the water. If you are entering from a height and don't want a bloody nose from face-planting on your surfboard, toss your board in ahead of you or hold your board to the side. Before launching, prearrange a time to check in with the boat so you aren't left out there for hours. Keep an eye on the boat in case the captain decides to move to another break earlier than planned.

OK!

BALANCING ON YOUR SURFBOARD

Once you are beyond the shorebreak the next step is to paddle outside, beyond where the waves are breaking. This crucial but challenging step is similar to the uphill climb on your mountain bike or skinning up to the top of your favorite backcountry ski run.

To paddle efficiently, you have to be balanced both front and back and left and right. Lie on your board so the nose of the board is an inch or less out of the water.

If your weight is too far back, the lowered tail will act like a sea anchor or an emergency break, dramatically slowing your surfboard.

If your weight is too far forward, your surfboard will plow through the water instead of gliding. In addition, when you try to catch a wave, the nose of your board will submerge, or pearl—a rather dramatic wipeout. New surfers who want to avoid such acrobatics often overcompensate and paddle with their weight too far back, making it difficult to catch anything except whitewater.

Once you have found your balance point, find a reference point on your surfboard such as a sticker on the deck or the feel of your leash plug on your feet. To make sure you are balanced left and right, center your head and chest on the stringer and keep your feet and knees together. Many beginners sprawl their legs out over the sides like outriggers. Although this feels stable, the position makes it impossible to paddle efficiently.

Just Right

surfboard nose about 1" above the water

your nose over a reference point on your surfboard

legs together and along centerline

Too Far Back

submerged tail of surfboard acts like an anchor

Too Far Forward

surfboard nose too close to or in the water

pearling on a wave

Paddling

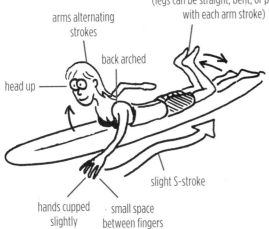

legs together and along centerline
(legs can be straight, bent, or pumped
with each arm stroke)

arms alternating
strokes

back arched

head up

hands cupped
slightly

small space
between fingers

slight S-stroke

use the double-handed paddle stroke only for short
bursts of speed (good for about two strokes)

if your head and chest are pressed against the surfboard deck,
it is harder to paddle with your arms
(this is also called the "dying cockroach" stroke)

The best posture for paddling is with your back arched and your head up looking forward, as opposed to lying completely flat on the board with your forehead pressed against the deck. This arched position makes it easier for your shoulders and arms to paddle. Paddle by alternating arm strokes, replicating the crawl, or freestyle, stroke. The simultaneous double-handed breaststroke is too tiring for normal paddling, so save it for last-ditch efforts to catch a wave. Cup your hands somewhat and keep your fingers slightly apart to maximize efficiency. Your legs (kept close together along the stringer) can either be straight, bent at the knee (easier on the back), or "pumped" to match your paddle strokes. Do whatever feels best for you.

knee paddling on a thick board
with lots of flotation

Surfers with particularly long and buoyant boards sometimes kneel on their board and paddle with both arms at the same time, similar to kneeling in the bottom of a canoe and propelling it with no paddle. This option gives other muscles a rest.

Sitting on Your Surfboard

Once you paddle to a calm area where no waves will bother you (usually outside the break), practice sitting up and lying down again. Sitting up and straddling your board with your legs enables you to better see and gauge what's coming and gives your neck, shoulders, and back a much-needed respite.

To sit up, push your torso upright and drop your legs on either side of the board.

You can sit with your board flat in the water or angled with the nose up like a missile launcher. Although sitting up with the board flat can be more comfortable and gives you a better view, sitting with the nose up is the quickest position to turn your surfboard around to catch a wave.

To adjust the angle of your board while sitting, push down on the deck between your legs and move the surfboard forward or backward a few inches at a time. The farther back you scoot your butt toward the tail, the deeper your tail sinks and the higher the nose of your surfboard will rise. You can balance with your board at about a 30-degree angle before you topple over backward. The board will tilt forward and back with the swells, so lean forward and backward as needed. To lie down again, reach up and grab the rails near the nose, then push the surfboard down between your legs the right amount as you lower yourself into paddling position. Make sure your legs are centered on the board. You can scoot your body forward or backward inchworm-like to make any final adjustments.

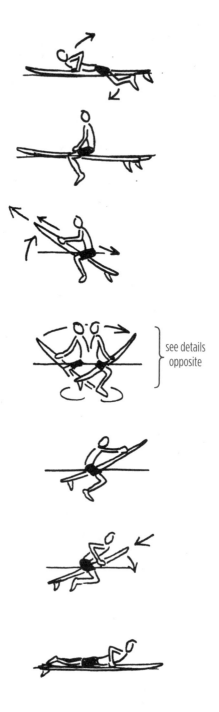

see details
opposite

Turning Your Surfboard

You need to know how to turn your board around quickly in order to catch a wave, as well as to maneuver around waves and other surfers while you are paddling out. For gradual turns while paddling, reach one hand out in the direction you want to go at a 45-degree angle from the nose and scoop the water toward the board while paddling normally with the other hand.

To turn in place, sit up on your surfboard and use your legs. Kick each leg in a circular, eggbeater motion in the same direction. To turn the board to the right, rotate both feet counterclockwise from the knee down, and vice versa to turn left. You can make sweeping strokes with your hands as well, but it is helpful to keep at least one hand on the rail of the board for balance.

For the fastest turns, scoot toward the rear of the surfboard so the nose is angled up, then use your legs as before (mind the fins on your ankles!). Once you are facing the direction you want to go, lie back down so you are ready to paddle again.

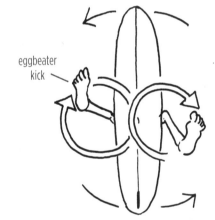

wide turn while
paddling forward

eggbeater
kick

turning with a flat surfboard

turning with the nose up

PADDLING THROUGH WAVES

The next obstacle is paddling through waves in the surf zone. When you check out the surf, look for channels around the breaking waves and other surfers. If at all possible, paddle around the whitewater instead of through it. Unbroken waves may look intimidating, but as long as they remain unbroken you can paddle over them fairly easily. As you crest over the wave, it may be helpful to hold one or both rails to steady yourself as you land on the other side. Never paddle out directly behind another surfer—if he/she loses their board, you are in its path.

Waves that have already broken or are in the act of breaking are much more difficult to paddle through. Breaking waves can knock you off your surfboard and drag you and your board back up the beach.

If an oncoming broken wave is small and you are still wading out, you can usually push your surfboard through it or lift the board up to the side over the whitewater. If you are already on your board, paddle hard to gain forward momentum and, just before you hit the whitewater, do a pushup so the whitewater goes between your body and the board.

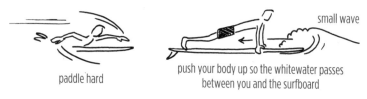

paddle hard

small wave

push your body up so the whitewater passes
between you and the surfboard

Turning Turtle

If the whitewater is thick and a good thrashing appears imminent, the best option is to turn turtle by flipping yourself and your board upside down, holding the rails tightly and using your body as a sea anchor as the wave washes over your board. Hold the board far enough from you to keep it from hitting you but close enough so you have some play in your arms. As you feel the whitewater begin to dissipate, turn the board back upright and climb on by flopping one leg on at a time (slower) or floating both legs to the surface and butterfly-kicking them up at the same time (quicker).

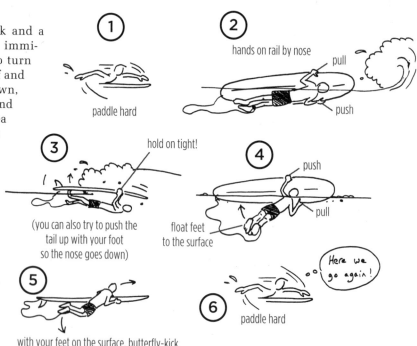

① paddle hard

② hands on rail by nose
pull
push

③ hold on tight!
(you can also try to push the tail up with your foot so the nose goes down)

④ push
float feet to the surface
pull

⑤ with your feet on the surface, butterfly-kick and pull yourself on your board

⑥ Here we go again!
paddle hard

Duck Diving on a Shortboard

Shortboarders and boogie boarders seem to magically dive under waves and pop up on the other side of the whitewater without losing their momentum. This maneuver, called **duck diving**, is extremely difficult on a buoyant longboard, but we'll review it here in case you make the transition to a shorter board.

Just before the whitewater hits you, grab the rails and straighten your arms to push your body up above the board so it sinks nose first. Place one foot on the tail to adjust the diving plane of the board (you can also use your knee, but it can ding your board). Lift the other leg above the water to keep sinking the board. Your body should sink below the surface just before the whitewater reaches you. As the whitewater passes above you, press down with your lower foot to sink the tail and at the same time pull up with your arms to raise the nose. Finally, push the board forward with your arms and return your legs to a centered paddling position. The upwardly angled board should surface in the calm water just beyond the whitewater. Resume paddling as you surface to avoid being dragged backward over the falls.

Duck diving is similar to rolling a kayak in that it seems effortless when everything is performed correctly but you will get thrashed if any part is done incorrectly. Common mistakes include not sinking deep enough before flattening out your surfboard, failing to angle upward, or rocketing up too soon. All result in the wave sucking you backward into the Maytag washer. Duck-diving through a steep wave face is much easier than duck-diving under whitewater on the flats because you don't need to dive as deep.

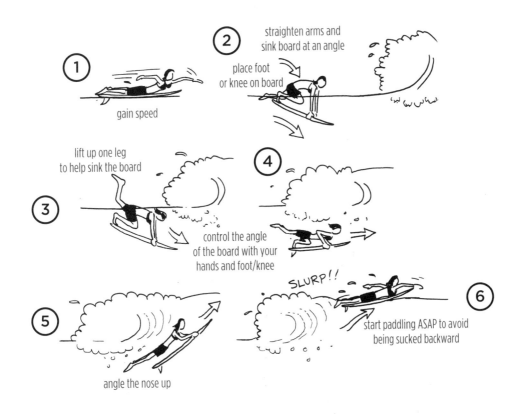

1. gain speed

2. straighten arms and sink board at an angle
place foot or knee on board

3. lift up one leg to help sink the board

4. control the angle of the board with your hands and foot/knee

5. angle the nose up

6. SLURP!! start paddling ASAP to avoid being sucked backward

Bailing

The most dangerous thing you can do when paddling out is to bail or abandon your surfboard while you duck under the oncoming wave. Although this may be the only course of action from time to time, use this option as a last resort. If you have to bail, make sure that no one is behind you, then duck underwater and try to swim below the turbulence. To minimize the chance of the lip breaking your board in half, turn your board parallel with the wave (boards don't break down the centerline very often).

If someone is behind you, turn turtle and hold on to your board. You may be surprised by the size of the wave that you are able to successfully turn turtle through.

Yikes!

Looks clear behind me! *

Good luck, board!

push board parallel with wave to reduce changes of the board breaking

duck and swim deep

* if it is *not* clear behind you, turn turtle and hold on to the board instead

Recovering in the Soup

At some point early in your career, a wave will wrench your surfboard away from you as you are paddling out, and you'll go for a spin cycle in the Maytag washer (a). Wait several long moments before you surface, and hold your arms over your head and face in case the board comes zinging back at you (b).

If you don't have enough time to climb back on your board before the next wave breaks on you, you may have to leave your board unclaimed and swim for the bottom (c). Do not grab onto the fin of the board or wrap the leash around your hand, because the next wave can yank away the board (and any entangled body parts). If the oncoming wave is particularly small, or if someone is directly behind you, you might be able to hold the board by the rail-saver section of the leash while you duck under, but always make sure you can let go of the leash if needed.

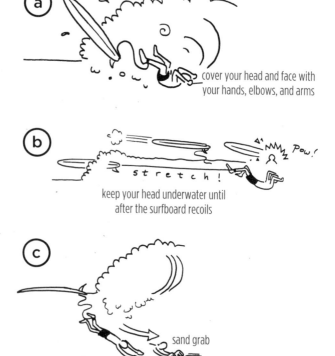

(a) cover your head and face with your hands, elbows, and arms

(b) stretch! Pow! keep your head underwater until after the surfboard recoils

(c) sand grab

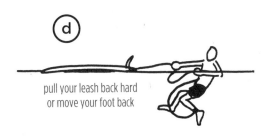

(d) pull your leash back hard
or move your foot back

(e) Time to paddle!

regain control
of the surfboard *quickly*

As soon as you have a chance, use your hands or your leg to pull the board back to you by the leash (d). Turn the board right side up, grab both rails, and slice the tail underneath you so the board is facing in the direction you want to go. (e) Climb on and start paddling. Even if you have to turn turtle with the very next wave, it is usually worth it to climb back on your board and make as much progress as you can. Just a few feet can make the difference between getting outside and getting washed all the way back to the beach.

For comparison purposes, let's follow Bailing Brenda, Turtling Tina, and Duck-Diving Diane and watch their wave coping techniques. Duck-Diving Diane dodges all the turbulence and keeps her forward momentum. Although the whitewater gives Turtling Tina a good thrashing and pushes her backward, she holds on to her board and is able to climb back on quickly and keep paddling. Bailing Brenda manages to escape the initial impact by diving deep, but her board yanks her back into the mayhem. Now she has to take the extra steps of retrieving and climbing on her board and making up a lot of lost ground before the next wave comes. If a set of waves is coming, she'll find it hard to make any forward progress.

Bailing Brenda =

Turtling Tina =

Duck-Diving Diane = (on a shortboard)

Making It through the Impact Zone

The **impact zone** is the last major obstacle to making it outside. The impact zone is the area where the largest waves break and release all their energy. Also called the Zona Impacta or the Boneyard, this is not a place to hesitate or linger. If you see an opening between sets, sprint out before the next set comes. If a set is looming, it may be wiser to hold your ground in the soup where the waves have

I think I'll wait here.

Time to sprint!

or*

facing the wave, nose down

back to the wave, with tail down

The Impact Zone

moves closer to shore with smaller waves and farther out with bigger waves

Wait Here for a Lull

*Note: two surfers should never be this close to one another in the whitewater

expended most of their energy and wait for the next lull before paddling out farther. To hold your position in small whitewater, sit up so the nose of the board is angled down and is slightly underwater,

then drop your legs so they act like sea anchors and let the wave splash over you. Another option is to spin and face the beach and do the same thing sitting on the very tail of the board. Or just turn turtle.

ⓐ ⓑ ?!! ⓒ ⓓ ⓔ

Avoiding Other Surfers on the Paddle Out

Riding waves is difficult enough without having to worry about steering around other people. The best way to stay out of the way of oncoming surfers is to paddle around the break instead of through it where other surfers will be riding the waves ⓐ. If a wave is breaking in front of you and no one is surfing on it or near you, paddle over the unbroken shoulder to avoid the whitewater ⓑ. If someone is already surfing on that wave and it looks as though your paths might cross, resist the urge to race them to the shoulder to avoid getting worked by the whitewater. This strategy dramatically increases the chances of a collision

ⓒ. Instead, paddle deliberately *into* the whitewater so you stay out of the other surfer's way ⓔ. The whitewater is the one place where you know that the other surfer does not want to be. Yes, you will probably get munched and perhaps be caught inside for the rest of the set, but this is preferable to having a collision or ruining someone's ride. Lastly, if oncoming surfers have an idea of where you are going, it will be easier for them to avoid you. Make your intentions known by paddling consistently. Avoid freezing like a deer in headlights or scrambling back and forth like a squirrel in front of a car ⓓ.

BEING OUTSIDE

Once you are outside the surf zone, the first thing to do is take ten more strokes just to make sure you are out far enough. Then concentrate on catching your breath instead of catching waves. Rest up a short distance away from the pack of other surfers to ensure that you are still out of everyone's way. Always keep your eye on the ocean and on the other surfers for cues. If someone whistles or yells "outside," that means a larger set is approaching, everyone is in danger of getting caught inside, and it's time to sprint out farther.

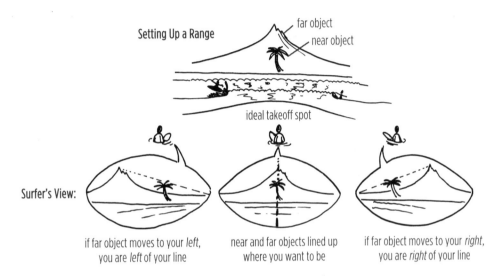

Setting Up a Range

far object
near object
ideal takeoff spot

Surfer's View:

if far object moves to your *left*, you are *left* of your line

near and far objects lined up where you want to be

if far object moves to your *right*, you are *right* of your line

Since other surfers have been waiting some time for a wave, it is considered proper etiquette to let other surfers have the next few waves before you paddle for one of your own. This also gives you additional time to watch how the waves are breaking. See more etiquette tips in Chapter 4 so you don't wear out your welcome.

While you are catching your breath, figure out what your position is along the shore and your distance out from shore. Although it is possible to use the other surfers gathered at the peak to keep track of your position, if everyone catches a wave or gets caught inside, it will be hard to figure out where you need to be. The best thing to do is **triangulate** your position. Line up a fixed object on shore with an object farther behind it. Sea kayakers and sailors

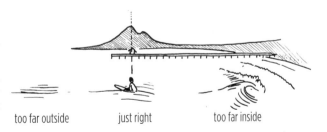

too far outside   just right   too far inside

If You Can, Also Set Up a Range to the Side So You Can Tell How Far Out You Are

refer to this line of position as a **range**. Ideally you can set up two ranges close to 90 degrees apart so you can also gauge your distance out from shore. If the far object moves to the right, you are moving to the right of your chosen line, and vice versa. Adjust your ranges as the break changes with the tide.

GETTING BACK TO SHORE

When coming back in, check to see if you are heading back to the same place you left from. If not, make sure that where you are heading is an acceptable option. Ideally, you ride a wave back to shore, but sometimes you have to swallow your pride and paddle in without a wave. Far too many surfers have spent an hour or more trying to catch one last wave so they didn't have to paddle for thirty seconds back to shore. Instead, think "three more waves," and just ride the next wave in to shore. Even if you can't catch a green wave, keep your eyes open for opportunities to belly-ride the whitewater in.

If you do manage to catch a wave in, you want to **kick out** (steer off the wave) or stall (slow down)

and then sit down so the wave passes you by (see page 153 in Chapter 6) before you reach the shore break. If you are belly-riding in, shift your weight toward the tail so you don't pearl. To stop, scoot your weight farther back, sit up, and drop your legs on either side of the board as sea anchors.

Another option on small waves is to angle your board sideways into the whitewater, lift the shoreward rail with one hand, and drag the other hand under the wave. As a last resort, flop backward off the board and into the whitewater before you reach the shore break.

waiting for "one more wave" invariably results in the surf going flat

when riding the soup in, scoot back on the board to avoid pearling

sit on the tail of the board and pull up the nose to stop (or bail off the back)

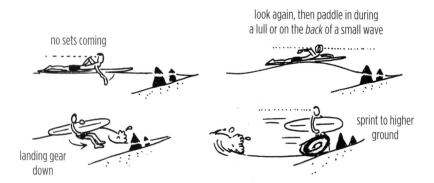

no sets coming

look again, then paddle in during a lull or on the *back* of a small wave

landing gear down

sprint to higher ground

To get through the shore break, wait for a break between larger waves and paddle in the rest of the way during the lull or on the surge of a small wave. Slip off the board and put down your landing gear as the surge brings you into the shallows (staying behind the wave crest as you land). Hustle up the beach before the next wave comes. Always keep your eye on the next wave.

If your timing is off and you find yourself about to be pummeled against the rocks by a sneaker wave, you have a couple of options. Your first choice should be to ⓐ paddle back out over the wave with your surfboard or ⓑ duck-dive under the wave if you can. Another deepwater option is to ⓒ duck under the wave and let your board take the beating.

The other strategy is to ⓓ sprint for higher ground (which always takes longer than you think). If you are unable to do this, another alternative is to let the wave break and then try to ⓔ jump over the whitewater, with your surfboard if possible. You can also ⓕ tuck behind a prominent rock, play barnacle, and hope for the best. If a wave pries you off the rock, tuck into a ball and cover your head (but don't plant your foot too firmly between rocks when a wave is approaching—broken ankles are the result).

As soon as you regain your footing and control of your board, retreat to deeper water or scramble to higher ground. If your leash becomes tangled, release it using the quick-release tab, retreat to safer ground, and retrieve your surfboard later.

never turn your back on the ocean

RESCUES

Here are some guidelines if you find yourself in over your head (literally and figuratively). Your surfboard is a wonderful flotation device and makes you much more visible, so sticking with it is a pretty good idea. Remember that this is not a first-aid or lifesaving book. Become a strong swimmer, learn CPR, and take first-aid and lifesaving courses and yearly refresher classes.

Rescuing Yourself

Even though you should always surf with a buddy and at a beach with a lifeguard on duty, you cannot rely on the lifeguard or your surf buddy to rescue you. You are ultimately on your own. It can be extremely hard for others to notice that you are in trouble or to do something about it in a timely fashion. Plan on taking care of yourself out there. A strong swimming ability is essential.

What to do if your leash breaks and you lose your surfboard. There are two types of surfers: those who have lost their surfboards and those who will. When your leash breaks, the strategy is usually pretty simple: swim and retrieve your board. This is where having a good foundation in bodysurfing is extremely helpful. Catching a wave in can save you lots of swim time. Inevitably and repeatedly, the next wave will reach your surfboard just before you do and wash it in farther.

If you lose sight of your board, just follow the whitewater in and ask other surfers if they saw where your board went. If your board washes into the cliffs or is blown offshore, you may want to amend your plans and swim to the safest shore.

Rip current refresher (see page 63 in Chapter 2 for a reminder). If you find yourself riding a rip current unintentionally, remember that a rip current is a relatively narrow stream of water rushing seaward. Instead of swimming against it, swim parallel to the shore until you are out of this current, then swim toward the shore.

Getting Yourself Rescued

If you find yourself in need of assistance, don't be shy. The universal signal for help is waving one hand over your head. Yelling is also appropriate, but be careful not to get a mouth full of water. Help can be a long way off, so signal for help *before* you are completely exhausted.

the safest way to shore may not be the shortest

when *not* to swim after your surfboard

rip current reminder: swim to the side

Be aware of your surroundings and where you are drifting. Usually the waves wash you into shore anyway. If you are seriously injured or along a dangerous shoreline, it may actually be safer to stay in deep water or swim farther out beyond the surf zone and wait for professional help to come to you in the form of a rescue tube, rescue board, personal watercraft, or boat. Pay close attention to any and all directions given to you.

Rescuing Others

You may also come across swimmers (more likely) or other surfers (less likely) in trouble. Keep in mind that you don't want to get yourself in trouble as well, so assess the situation before you rush in to save someone. You can also be helpful by keeping your distance, alerting others, and keeping track of someone's position until rescuers arrive.

Returning a lost surfboard.

If a surfer loses her surfboard, the waves will often wash it onto the beach. The first things you should do if you see a lost, out-of-control board careening toward you is get out of the way and warn others around you. Do not put yourself in harm's way to rescue another board, but it is considered good karma to help out if you can do so safely. At a minimum, keep an eye on the surfer swimming in to make sure she doesn't have any

paddle to the side of an oncoming lost surfboard

between sets, climb on the lost board, keeping your own leash on

Thanks!

No worries!

paddle out to meet the other surfer, towing your own surfboard behind you

trouble, and point her in the direction of the board if needed. If you are on the beach and the board washes up to you, carry it up the beach and away from the pounding shore break.

If you are in the water and the board comes to rest between waves, you can save the surfer a long swim if you intercept the board before the next set comes in. First, wait until the board is completely free of a wave before you paddle up to it, and make sure you have time before the next wave comes through. Be aware that a breaking wave that reaches the board before you do will convert the board into a battering ram. With your leash on, slip off your own board, climb onto the drifting board, and let your own board float behind you toward shore. Next, paddle the rescued board out to the other surfer, towing your board behind you on your leash, or wait in a safe place for the surfer to swim to you. If someone loses his board while you are outside and you are feeling truly generous, you can catch the next wave in and try to catch the board between waves.

Rescuing a swimmer.
A panicky swimmer can be just as dangerous as a rip current. Do not give him an opportunity to climb on top of you and sit on your head, which is his initial thought. The first thing to do is to get the swimmer's attention and give him verbal directions in a calm but commanding voice from a safe distance. If you do not feel comfortable assisting directly, signal for help. The most direct way to help out is to paddle up to him, slip off your board (before you come within thrashing distance) so your board is between you and him, and extend the board to him. Direct him to hold on to the board or, if he is capable, climb onto the board. While he catches his breath and calms down, continue to talk to him while you either signal for help or tow him to shore. If you have a long enough board and he is calm, you can climb on behind him and help him paddle to shore. If the swimmer is on a short board, you can hold on to the tail and kick toward shore. Ask the person his name and use it often.

Here... calm down and grab on to my board!

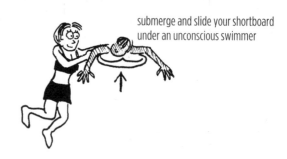

submerge and slide your shortboard under an unconscious swimmer

Rescuing an incapacitated swimmer. You can help an incapacitated or unconscious swimmer by slipping your surfboard under them. If you have a shortboard or boogie board, you can sink the board underneath him and guide it as it floats up to support him.

If you have a longboard, here's a neat trick to help haul a swimmer onto your board.

(1) Paddle your board a few feet from the swimmer, then slip off and flip your board upside down. (2) Reach across the center of your overturned board and grab his wrists. (3) Pull his arms across your board until his head and shoulders reach the stringer of the board. (4) Grab his wrist with one hand and (5) push down your side of the board as you grab its far edge and flip the board over toward you. Use your weight to turn the board back upright so his chest is resting on the board. Putting your knee on your board may help flip it. The person should now be facedown across your upright board. (6) Reach across and grab his closest leg, then pivot his torso so his body is in line with your board and his head is out of the water. (7) You might need to scoot him forward or backward, or center him for better balance on the board. (8) Now you can either tow him with a sidestroke or, if there is room, have him spread him legs, then climb onto the board with him and paddle to shore.

If you don't feel comfortable bringing him through the surf zone, or if the landing zone isn't safe, another option is to swim farther outside so you are both beyond the break. Lifeguards with access to a boat, rescue watercraft, or rescue board can more easily transport an injured person back to shore or to a harbor. Signal for help by waving your arm above your head. Because a boat-based rescue may take some time to initiate, stay as calm as you can, talk to the swimmer in need, and save your energy.

(1) flip surfboard over

(2) grab swimmer's wrists

(3) pull swimmer across overturned surfboard

(4) hold one wrist and grab the far edge of the board

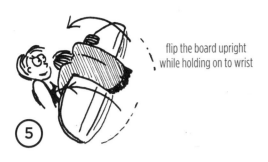

flip the board upright while holding on to wrist

pivot swimmer's legs on the board

center swimmer on the board

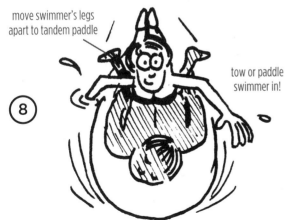

move swimmer's legs apart to tandem paddle

tow or paddle swimmer in!

CPR, Artificial Respiration, First-Aid, and Lifesaving Skills

All surfers should know when and how to perform the current versions of cardiopulmonary resuscitation (CPR) and artificial respiration and know basic first-aid and rescue skills. The Red Cross, local fire departments, and United States Lifesaving Association (www.usla.org) are great resources. Although it is possible to perform artificial respiration while someone is still in the water, CPR must be performed on the shore or in a rescue boat. Some local businesses, such as Surfpulse in northern California, sponsor surf rescue courses offered by local fire departments and harbor patrols. These courses cover the techniques presented here in greater detail. Techniques for all these skills are constantly evolving, so learn the most current versions. Reading about these skills is no replacement for taking a class and practicing.

Preventing Rescues in the First Place

The first thing to do to is to prevent your own rescue by not becoming a victim. Use the clues in Chapter 2 to choose an appropriate location for surfing, look for warning signs of places to avoid, and steer clear of those "sick barrels breaking on a dry reef!" If you find yourself in over your head, survey the scene and choose the safest retreat (it may not be the nearest retreat). Don't be afraid to ask for help from others around you.

It's easier to prevent a rescue than perform one. If you see a clueless swimmer or a beginning surfer who is oblivious to some hazard, politely give him a heads-up and keep an eye on him until he is out of harm's way.

Surf Etiquette

4

"We are very lucky to be surfers—Share the water."

—Tribal Law, Surfrider's Code of Ethics

Congratulations! Hopefully by now you are bobbing in the lineup outside the impact zone and have marked your position with a couple of ranges on shore. Before you can start catching waves, though, you need to understand the rules of the road. Surf etiquette is an issue not only of civility but of safety. Aside from rip currents and rocks, the most dangerous things out there are surfboards (your own and other surfers'). Although these rules of the road may be somewhat frustrating for beginner surfers, understanding them is key to fitting in with other surfers and safely catching more waves.

"Surfers? We're a mob of greedy, adrenalin-fueled colonials participating in an unbelievably frustrating activity that drags out our worst instincts."

—Derek Rielly in *Surf Rage*, by Nat Young

"Whether we like it or not, we surfers are part of a culture which seems to be increasingly competitive, reflecting the frustrations of this very crowded planet on which we live."

—Nat Young, *Surf Rage*

"Give respect to get respect."
—Tribal Law, Surfrider's Code of Ethics

"A local is someone who's been there a day longer than you."

—Derek Rielly in *Surf Rage*, by Nat Young

LOCALISM VS. ALOHA SPIRIT

Localism is a form of territoriality that local surfers have for their home surf breaks. It can range from a somewhat positive sense of pride in a local break and surf buddies to outright paranoid xenophobia. Localism is a result of local surfers running out of patience as hordes of visiting surfers clog up formerly uncrowded waves in their neighborhood. In addition to having to compete for waves, the failure of other surfers to practice proper etiquette doesn't help. The biggest frustrations often relate to visitors using longboards or stand-up paddleboards to take more than their fair share of waves, outsiders **dropping in** on local surfers (see page 109), and tourons just getting in the way out there.

Locals figured out that the best way to keep the waves to themselves is to try to intimidate the other surfers from surfing there. Giving the stink eye, verbal abuse, smashed windows, flattened tires, personal threats, and physical violence are all expressions of localism. At certain places, even surfers who have spent years surfing a break are not yet "true locals" and are still at the bottom of

"stink eye"

the pecking order. Although localism does instill a form of Darwinian order in the lineup and can deter crowds, recent episodes of violence have highlighted the ugly side of surfing and caused some reflection in the surfing community.

In contrast to localism, surfers can also exhibit the "aloha spirit." Born from the rich Hawaiian beach culture, aloha spirit is a form of graciousness and generosity in the water. The idea behind this is that waves are a renewable resource, and if everyone follows the rules and isn't greedy, there are plenty of waves for everyone. Examples of the aloha spirit include telling a newcomer the best place to paddle out, letting someone else have a chance at a wave, and saying "nice wave" after a surfer has an exceptional ride.

Do your part to diffuse localism and instill the aloha spirit by following surf etiquette, showing common courtesy, and letting the person next to you have the occasional wave. Deferring to locals on the choicest waves helps a lot, too.

RULES FROM THE BEACH

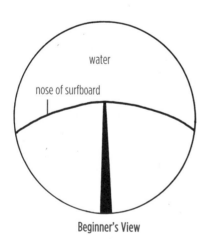

water

nose of surfboard

Beginner's View

Don't Bring a Crowd

Don't show up at a surf spot with ten of your best buddies and expect a warm welcome. It's far easier to work your way into the lineup if it's just you and a friend.

Be Aware of Your Surroundings

These rules work only if you are aware of your surroundings and are looking, listening, and learning. Like beginning drivers fixated on the hood of the car, newbie surfers often have tunnel vision and focus only on the nose of their board. Be aware of your surroundings and what other surfers are doing. Learn to look left, right, and straight ahead before dropping in on a wave, and learn to hold on to your board at all times. Listen for a whistle or hoot (the equivalent of a horn) warning you that you didn't see someone, and be ready and able to kick out, pull back, or paddle out of the way.

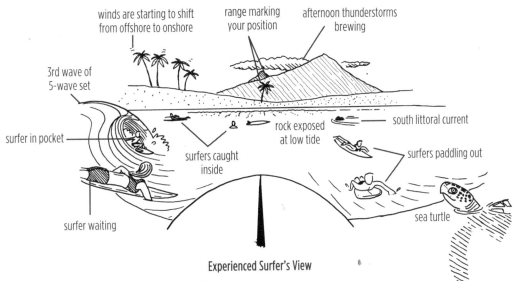

winds are starting to shift from offshore to onshore

range marking your position

afternoon thunderstorms brewing

3rd wave of 5-wave set

surfer in pocket

surfers caught inside

rock exposed at low tide

south littoral current

surfers paddling out

surfer waiting

sea turtle

Experienced Surfer's View

Select an Appropriate Place to Surf

The first lesson in surfing etiquette is to locate a surf break that is within your ability. Student drivers shouldn't start off learning how to drive in Los Angeles rush hour or in the Daytona 500, but instead should seek out an empty parking lot after hours. Use the guidelines on page 68 in Chapter 2 to select a good beach break for beginners. Look for small, gently spilling waves, multiple peaks, and a lifeguard on duty. When in doubt, don't go out.

Hold on to Your Surfboard

...as a ride ends

...when you wipeout

...when paddling out through a wave

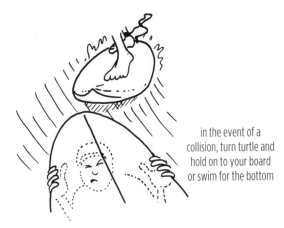

in the event of a collision, turn turtle and hold on to your board or swim for the bottom

Stay Out of the Way of Oncoming Surfers

When paddling out, paddle around the waves and out of the path of other surfers. If a surfer is riding a wave toward you, paddle for the whitewater and turn turtle instead of paddling toward the unbroken shoulder. If you sprint toward the shoulder to avoid the whitewater, you will interfere with the surfer's ride and risk a collision (see p. 109 for details).

Even though experienced surfers can often maneuver around other surfers fairly easily, all it takes for a collision is for one surfer to be in the wrong place at the wrong time. If someone is about to run you over, the best thing to do is to turn turtle or swim for the bottom.

RULES IN THE LINEUP

Wait in the Right Spot

One sure way to generate ill will is to paddle right into the middle of a pack of surfers who have been waiting for a set, and then catch the very next wave. A better approach is to wait off to the side and watch to see how the break and crowd rotation work. Plan on passing on the first set of waves and watching how and where the other surfers are catching waves.

After the original surfers have caught a wave and cycled through, you can insert yourself in position. It is better to start out catching the side

peaks or leftover waves, leaving the choice set waves for those who were there first.

Only when you feel comfortable with the conditions and the other surfers should you move on to the main peak. You should be aware that at some popular breaks, local surfers consider the main peak to be "reserved" for their use only, and paddling here will earn you the stink eye, or worse. Sometimes it's better to be content with the side peaks, particularly as a beginner.

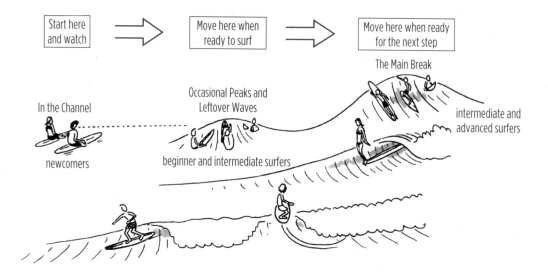

One Person on a Wave at a Time

Surfing's most basic rule is one person at a time on a wave. Riding a wave is not only safer when only one surfer is on it, it is much more enjoyable that way. A wave is like a blank canvas. Whether your wave ends up being a two-second or a two-minute ride, it's your wave to do with as you like. You are free to cut back, speed down the line, go for some crazy maneuver, or zen out and soak it all in. More than one surfer on a wave mars the wave for the first surfer. (Note: If a wave breaks in both directions, it is possible for two surfers to "split" the peak, so each has a wave face to surf.)

Don't Drop In on Another Surfer

While "dropping in" means catching a wave, "dropping in *on*" someone means catching and standing up on a wave already occupied by another surfer. Dropping in on another surfer is the equivalent of drunk driving through a red light in a school zone. The surfer who catches the wave first is usually at the steepest and fastest part of the wave, while a surfer who catches the wave second is usually closer to the slower shoulder off to the side. Even though the second surfer may be some distance from the first surfer, the first surfer will have much more speed and will quickly be able to catch up with the surfer who dropped in. "Dropping in" on someone is also called "burning" him or her, or "shoulder hopping."

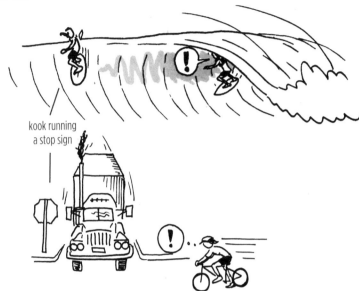

kook running a stop sign

One exception to the previous rule is during crowded conditions on wide, gently breaking waves that constantly re-form as they roll toward shore. These are generally beginner or longboarder breaks where the waves break too gently to be ridden on a shortboard. Because of the way these waves break, the whitewater stays near the top of the wave, leaving everyone with a green face to ride for an extended time. If everyone is riding straight toward shore, another surfer a few feet to your left or right does not interfere with the wave or with your ride. You may see ten or more surfers on the same wave. Classic breaks where you may see this phenomenon include Cowell's Beach in Santa Cruz, California; Old Man's Beach in San Onofre, California; and Waikiki Beach on the island of Oahu in the Hawaiian Islands.

How do you know whether or not it's okay to join other surfers on a wave? Check to see whether everyone else is surfing straight in instead of angling across the wave and be sure you can join them without getting in anyone else's way. Someone angling across the wave toward you is a sign that you should let that person have the wave or kick out if you are already in the wave. A "party wave" is a call made by a person with the right of way inviting her friends to join her on a wave.

First Person up Has the Right-of-Way*

There are usually more surfers in the water than surfable waves per set, so not everyone will catch a wave in every set. If everyone stood up on every wave they paddled for and caught, there would be more than one person on each wave, and the waves would be overcrowded and dangerous.

So how do surfers decide who gets to take a wave? Because of the physics of catching a wave, the first person standing is usually at the biggest and fastest part of the wave. If the other people are riding standup paddleboards, boogie boards, kneeboards, or kayaks, the first person to stop paddling and start planing has the right-of-way. This person has in effect won that lottery and has that wave all to herself. Surfers position themselves where they think the wave is going to break first so they can be the first one standing.

*Fast Craft Need to Go Slow

This basic rule becomes more complicated if a variety of surf craft is in the lineup. Because of their faster hull speed, kayakers, standup paddleboarders, and longboarders can catch a given wave much earlier than shortboarders, bodyboarders, or bodysurfers.

Since the "first person up has the right of way," and longboards can catch waves farther outside than shortboards, technically, a longboarder could always catch a wave before a shortboarder, and thus the shortboarder could never ride a wave following this rule. Longboards also paddle faster than shortboards, so those on a longboard could race back out to get more than their fair share of waves. Overenthusiastic kayakers, longboarders, and standup paddleboard surfers have earned the resentment of otherwise patient shortboarders. Surfers on faster craft need to exercise some restraint and let some quality waves go by so other surfers farther in can catch some waves of their own.

Person Closest to Curl Has Right of Way

What if two people stand up at exactly the same time? The person closest to the curl, peak, or breaking part of the wave has the right of way. This is also the steepest and fastest part of the wave, so the surfer catching a wave here will soon outrace a person farther toward the shoulder.

There is a potential point of confusion if the first person up is farther over on the shoulder and the next person standing is closest to the curl. Who has the right of way? If both surfers catch the wave and stand up anywhere near the same time, **the person closest to the peak has the right of way.** The longer the first person up has been riding that wave, the greater his or her claim to the wave despite another person's later position closer to the curl. Once a surfer is riding a wave, it is not acceptable for another surfer to catch a wave between the first surfer and the whitewater to claim the wave.

Splitting the Peak

If a wave breaks both left and right, a surfer can go in each direction and still have the wave to his or herself. If you are on a peak and can go in either direction, it is considered respectful if you call out which way you are going so other nearby surfers have the option of surfing the wave in the other direction. Consider "splitting the peak" with the other surfer so you both catch a wave, even if that means giving the other person the better ride.

right of way

needs to kick out

right of way going right   right of way going left

right of way

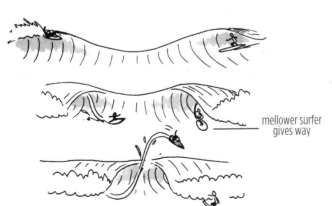

mellower surfer gives way

If someone is taking off deeper than you (closer to the peak or behind the peak), they have the right of way.

Dealing with Different Peaks on the Same Wave

Two surfers coming toward each other on the same wave from two different peaks both have to yield. In the spirit of sharing waves, the less skilled surfer should straighten out or kick out earlier so the more advanced surfer who is making the most vertical moves can have a big finale.

Don't Snake

Snaking is jockeying for position for a wave at the last second to end up closest to the curl. Snaking is like jumping in front of your ski buddy as he adjusts his goggles so you get the first tracks on a powder day. Snaking is considered bad form and unnecessarily aggressive. Snaking is also dropping in on someone deliberately.

Another no-no, mentioned previously, is to wait until the standing surfer has passed you, and then catch the wave. While you might technically be closer to the curl at that point, the other surfer was up first and still has priority.

Don't Take Off in Front of Other Surfers Paddling Out

As much as surfers try to stay out of each other's way, sometimes a surfer ends up directly in the path of someone else riding a wave or trying to catch a wave. If you are about to take off and someone is in your way (even if it is the wave of the day!), you need to back off and let the wave pass. Although unfortunate, this happens to all surfers once in a while.

Likewise, if you are already riding a wave and someone who has not read this book paddles directly in your way, it is your duty to avoid the other surfer by steering around him, straightening out, kicking out, or wiping out.

"SO WHEN *CAN* I CATCH A WAVE?"

Luckily, there are several circumstances when you *can* catch a wave.

When No One Else Paddles for the Wave

Even on crowded days, a swell will occasionally bypass other surfers and head directly toward you. With the other surfers paddling out farther or taking a break, there is no doubt that this wave is all yours. Make the most of it!

If No One Farther Out Catches the Wave

Just because someone is paddling for a wave doesn't mean she will always catch it. In crowded conditions, it can be prudent to be ready to paddle for a wave or be paddling and ready to stand up just in case the other person doesn't catch it. Just make sure you are not in her way in case she catches the wave. This does not have to be an aggressive move. If she misses the wave and you catch it, then there's one less surfer in a lineup for the next set, decreasing the waiting time for everyone. Likewise, if you are paddling for a wave and realize you are going to miss it, let any other surfers lining up for it know and encourage them to go for it.

If the Other Surfer Wipes Out

If the other person wipes out, the wave is fair game for the next person closest to the curl. Again, it can be strategic to be ready to paddle for a wave in just in case the wave opens up. Don't drop in unless you actually see the other person wipe out. Nimble surfers can surprise you with a gravity-defying save. Never paddle for a wave while a surfer is still up and riding. You can ruin his ride by causing the section of wave you are on to break prematurely.

If the Other Surfer Kicks Out

Sometimes surfers kick out of a wave before it is completely finished breaking, leaving a still surfable wave. Usually surfers kick out at the end of a particularly exciting section or as the wave flattens out. These "leftovers" or "crumbs" can still be great waves as long as you stay out of the way of surfers riding all the way through. Sometimes these mushy waves re-form and have exciting inside sections.

If the Other Surfer Goes in the Other Direction

As described on page 111, if the surfer goes in the other direction, the wave is fair game. It is polite to call out ahead of time which way you are going so other surfers can surf the other direction.

If the Wave Closes Out and the Surfer Can't Make It Out of the Whitewater

In this case, always give the other surfer the benefit of the doubt. You will be amazed how fast a surfer (particularly on a shortboard) can travel on a wave that looked as though it was going to break all at once (a). It may appear that the wave has closed out when someone is really in the tube (b). If you decide to drop in, you could land on her head (bad) and ruin her ride (worse). At this point in your surfing career, before dropping in make sure you actually see that the other surfer has deliberately bailed out or resigned himself to the whitewater. Even if you are certain that he didn't make it around a section and you decide to drop in, still look for him and be ready and able to kick out if he is still on the wave (c). When in doubt, don't drop in.

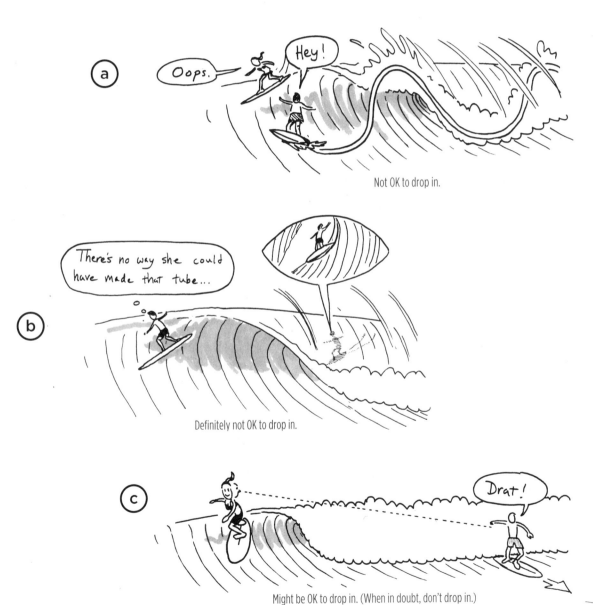

Not OK to drop in.

Definitely not OK to drop in.

Might be OK to drop in. (When in doubt, don't drop in.)

Wait Your Turn

Sometimes a small group of surfers will let the person waiting the longest have the next wave, or two groups of surfers at a remote break may alternate sessions so that there are fewer people in the water, but this is the exception rather than the rule.

The problem with waiting your turn is that surfers don't usually take turns. The reality of surfing is that experienced surfers repeatedly catch the biggest and best waves. Because these surfers can position themselves in the steeper, more challenging takeoff zone where the wave first breaks, they claim priority and have the wave to themselves, leaving beginners bobbing surflessly out on the wave shoulders for hours. This hierarchy might not feel fair (particularly if you are a beginner), but it is the natural pecking order.

The good news is that you don't need to just bob listlessly and wavelessly in the lineup. Instead, aim for the smaller waves or go to some less-competitive breaks where you can catch more waves.

Don't be a wave hog, but don't be flotsam, either.

Show Respect

Even if you already know how to surf and are a prodigious ripper, you need to show respect to get respect. If you follow the rules, you will get more deference on waves. If you really want to impress someone, take a pass on some choice waves and encourage someone else who is ready to take the wave. Other surfers will be more likely to return the favor. If you ignore the rules of the road, other surfers will assume you don't deserve to surf (even if you can) and will be more likely to hassle you.

Make Your Waves

There's no pressure here. NOT! On the bunny slope of surfing—the beginner break—no one cares whether or not you can already surf. Beginner breaks are places to sort things out and make all kinds of mistakes. Once you leave the bunny slope and head out to a "real" surf break, you are expected to have some basic skills.

Other surfers will be sizing you up to see if you know how to surf. If you wait your turn and successfully make the drop, angle, and kick out on your first wave, you will get some respect. If you clutch and pull back or wipe out on a perfectly decent wave, other surfers will assume that you can't surf. Not wanting to have the best wave of the day wasted because they think you are going to blow this one, too, other surfers may drop in on you.

This doesn't mean you can't challenge yourself and push your limits. If you don't wipe out often, you are not learning. Everyone blows it on the wave of the day at some point. If you follow proper etiquette and aren't too far over your skill level, other surfers will give you the space and encouragement to do it better the next time.

ENFORCEMENT OF THE RULES

Surfers expect other surfers to know the rules. There are no traffic cops, referees, or umpires to enforce them. Surfers usually follow a live and let live policy and are generally silent unless they themselves are affected. If someone gives you the stink eye, consider this a first warning: whatever you did, don't do it again. If a transgression is overt or repeated, surfers may use a more heavy-handed approach, with verbal reprimands or physical intimidation to get their point across.

What If You Break a Rule?

The most important thing to do is apologize at your first opportunity. A simple apology shows that you realize you made a mistake and won't do it again. Apologizing also helps maintain a positive vibe in the lineup.

What if You Accidentally Drop In on Someone?

If you accidentally drop in on someone, kick out as soon as you can so you are no longer on her wave. If you can't kick out, stay high on the wave, keep surfing toward the shoulder, and kick out as soon as you can. Try not to wipe out or shoot your board at the other surfer, and hold on to your board if possible.

What If Someone Drops In on You?

Experienced surfers sometimes drop in on beginners if it is apparent that the beginner will be trapped in the whitewater or be surfing straight in to the beach, leaving the unbroken face available. As you become more experienced and start surfing across the face of a wave, other surfers should give you more space.

Other beginning surfers may not know the rules of the road and unwittingly drop in on you and cut you off. If someone drops in on you, the best thing to do is to give a low-key whistle or hoot so he knows you are there and can kick out. If he is in danger of colliding with you, straighten out and keep control of your board. If other surfers knowingly keep dropping in on you and ruining your rides, you should probably call it a day at this spot.

If you notice a first timer flailing on the shoulder and are feeling generous, consider sharing your wave with him or letting him have the wave.

What if Your Board Hits Someone?

Check and make sure that you, the other person, and both boards are okay. Quickly disentangle any snarled leashes before the next wave comes. Obviously, help out if anyone is hurt. If the board bashing was your fault, offer to cover the cost of any ding repairs.

What if Someone Gives You a Hard Time?

You may find yourself receiving "unconstructive verbal feedback" at some point. If you made a mistake, apologize and then give the other person some space. If you did nothing to prompt the outburst, engaging in a conversation may escalate the situation. Do not be a smart-ass. Instead, just remove yourself from the situation.

5

Reading and Catching Waves

"... every wave is a masterpiece of originality. It will ever be so. Go and see."
—Willard Bascomb, *Waves and Beaches*

Congratulations! You are safe in the deep water outside of the break, which is surfing's equivalent to the top of the ski lift. You understand the difference between a rip current and undertow and know the rules of the road so you won't put yourself in harm's way or worse, ruin anyone else's ride. In this chapter you will learn the arts of reading waves and catching waves.

Catching waves really means catching the right waves, which means you need to be able "read" what type of wave is coming your way. Even at a beginner break, the ocean can still pitch any type of wave at you. There are the watery equivalents of fastballs, curveballs, sliders, knuckleballs, sinkers, spitballs, and beaners, and it is up to you to choose which ones to go for and which ones to let pass. The following gallery is a partial list of waves you are likely to encounter.

THE ROGUE WAVE GALLERY

The passive-aggressive wave. This wave looks gentle and easy, but it will double up, close out, and pitch you over the falls as soon as it hits the sandbar. Learn to recognize and avoid.

The tease. This fun-looking wave lures you into the impact zone and then disappears, setting you up to be clobbered by the next wave.

The rogue wave. An extremely large, atypical wave for that day.

The cleanup or sneaker set. A set of much bigger waves that breaks farther outside and catches almost everyone off-guard, pummeling them in the impact zone.

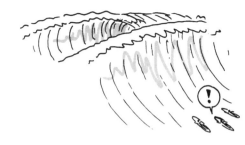

The shifty wave. This wave looks like it is going to break at one spot but the peak will shift to the side, leaving hopeful surfers flailing far out on the flat shoulder.

The wave of the day. A great wave, not to be repeated. Go for it!

The party wave. This is a wide, gentle wave at a beginner break where everyone rides straight toward shore (see *Surfin'ary* by Trevor Cralle).

The mushburger. This is a slow dribbling, spilling wave, perfect for beginners on longboards and reviled by shortboarders.

The peeler. A peeling wave breaks gradually along the wave face, allowing the surfer to carve across the wave face for a long ride.

The barrel. A plunging wave inside which skilled surfers can ride or get "tubed, barreled, or shacked."

The closeout. A wave that breaks all at once or dumps instead of peeling.

READING WAVES AND WAVE SELECTION: WHICH WAVE FOR YOU?

With time, you will be able to tell when and where a wave is going to break (farther out, farther in, or on top of your head), how a wave is going to break (spilling gently or pitching over onto your head), and whether the wave is going to peel or close out (on top of your head). The best way to learn how waves behave is to watch how different ones form and break and how surfers respond. Did anyone paddle for the wave? What happened to them? Then try it yourself and try to remember what happened.

Wide Surf Zone

For beginning beginners. For beginners, you want a small (knee to chest high), gently spilling wave that gives you plenty of time to paddle into it and stand up. You can either catch green (unbroken) wave or the whitewater from waves that have already broken. Because you are going to be riding straight into the beach, don't worry if the wave is going to close out or peel as long as it is a dribbler and not a dumper.

Beginners dealing with larger surf: catching the whitewater on the inside. On days with bigger (chest high and above) surf or pitching waves, beginners can still learn the basics by catching the subdued whitewater from waves that have already broken without ever venturing out into the big surf. The whitewater can also "reform" on the inside as green waves. Look for a stretch of whitewater that is far enough from the impact zone to be gentle and is still far enough from shore for you to have time to stand up. Be aware that you won't have as much time to rest and turn around as you would if you were outside the break.

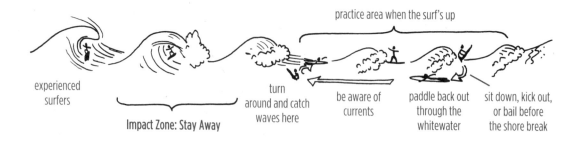

experienced surfers

Impact Zone: Stay Away

turn around and catch waves here

be aware of currents

practice area when the surf's up

paddle back out through the whitewater

sit down, kick out, or bail before the shore break

angling

straight to shore (the whitewater will soon catch up)

angling

Waves for your next session: catching green, peeling waves. Next-level beginners should paddle outside to catch unbroken or green waves. Look for gently breaking waves that peel instead of close out so you can angle across the face for a longer ride instead of just surfing in straight to shore. As your skills grow, you can paddle for larger waves, take off in the steeper, more critical parts of the wave, and try more maneuvers.

GETTING IN POSITION TO PADDLE FOR A WAVE

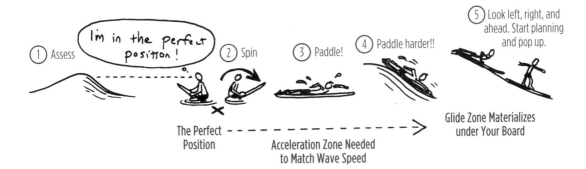

Now that you know which waves to paddle for and which ones to avoid, the next step is to be in proper position to paddle for a green wave and catch it. Sit up and reassess the wave as it approaches and be ready to spin. If it still looks good, turn your board around and paddle toward shore. Remember that you will still need an "acceleration zone" of 5–15 feet to build up enough speed to catch the wave. If all goes according to plan, the wave should overtake you, and the glide zone should form underneath you just when you reach cruising speed.

Waves provide instant feedback on your position (assuming you are paddling fast enough). If you are too far outside, the wave will pass you by. If you are too far inside, the wave will break on you and you will pearl.

The perfect position to wait for a wave changes with every wave. In some super-consistent places on super-consistent days, this varies by a only few feet from wave to wave. In most places, however, this position can change substantially with every wave—so you have to be ready to paddle. To avoid getting caught inside, most surfers sit just outside the ideal takeoff position and paddle in when they see a wave they want to catch.

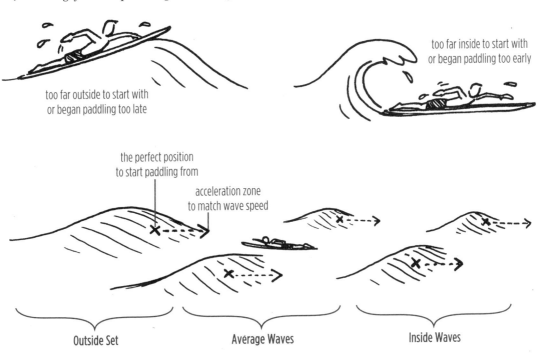

So if you never move, it can be a long time before a wave comes along that perfectly matches your position. If you are willing to paddle 25 feet to be in paddling position, you will catch many more waves. If you are willing and able to paddle 50 feet to be in paddling position for any given wave, you will be able to catch four times as many waves. (Of course, this means being able to read the wave well enough to know where you have to be.)

Sprinting Spike's wave-catching range

Barnacle Bill's wave-catching range

Paddle in toward shore. In this case the wave is going to break between you and the beach. This is the most common situation as surfers usually sit outside the impact zone to avoid being caught inside.

Spin around and start paddling as the wave approaches, but be aware that the wave shape may change while you are paddling. Before you catch the wave and stand up, look left, right, and ahead to make sure that this wave is still one you want to catch and that the coast is clear. If you have miscalculated, be ready to sit up on the surfboard and stop yourself.

spin

sprint

spin

Paddle out to the wave. If the wave is going to break farther out than you are, you have paddle farther out to meet the wave. The farther out you paddle, the less likely the wave is going to break on you, but the less time you will have to stop, spin, and build up speed to catch the wave. The sooner you stop and spin, the more time you will have to gain momentum, but the more likely the wave is going to break on your head.

spin

paddle out and then back in to where you were

Paddle out and then back in to the same spot. In this "should I stay or should I go?" scenario, you could probably stay exactly where you are but paddling out and back gives you added speed to catch the wave, room for error if the wave breaks early, as well as a psychological advantage. If you sit perfectly still, other surfers may assume that you aren't interested in the wave whereas if you are actively paddling for it they might give you priority.

Paddle to the side. In this case, you are the right distance out but the peak is off to one side. Spin 90 degrees and sprint to the peak. Once there, sit back up, spin 90 degrees toward shore, lay back down, and start paddling.

Sitting up not only helps you turn faster and easier, but also allows a surfer to better reassess a wave than by craning her neck and interpreting the wave from a prone position. In this way, sitting up is similar to a whale or seal spy hopping to get a better view.

sit up and "spy hop," then spin and sprint

shortcut with a prone turn

"Spy Hopping Seal"

Putting it all together. In many cases, you have to paddle in or out as well as to the side. If you have to turn 90 degrees or more, it is usually more efficient to sit up and spin and then lay back down again. If you have to turn 90 degrees or less and are comfortable with the wave, you can stay prone and do a more gradual turn while paddling.

With more experience, you will be better able to anticipate and move in position early so you have plenty of time to rest, reassess, and catch the wave. You will see experienced surfers paddle out to the middle of nowhere and, two minutes later, be in the perfect position for the wave of the day.

prone turn

sit up and spin turn

Where is she going?

I have no idea.

2 minutes later...

How did she do that?

CATCHING WAVES

Now that you are in the proper position to paddle for a wave, you have to connect with it. To catch a wave and start learning how to surf, you have to *want* it. Go for it with gusto. Don't think of "catching a wave" as in "catching up with a wave," because it is impossible to paddle faster than a wave. Instead, think about the wave catching up with you and where you want to be when it does.

without speed

Catching a wave is like jumping onto a moving train. You first try to match the speed of the passing boxcar so you can grab hold and leap on board just when the open boxcar door catches up with you. The window for matching the speed of the wave is fairly small. If you paddle too slowly or too late, the wave will pass you by. If you paddle too fast or too early, you will paddle past the glide zone and on into the impact zone, where the wave will be breaking.

with speed

With practice, you will sprint toward shore just as the wave's glide zone appears directly beneath you. The wave needs to be steep enough for your board to start sliding downhill but not so steep that the wave crest starts sliding down with you as well. Remember that longboards plane more easily than short-boards, so longboarders can catch waves well before they steepen and break. Shortboards don't start planing until the wave is much steeper, so shortboard-ers have to wait until the wave starts breaking in order to catch the wave.

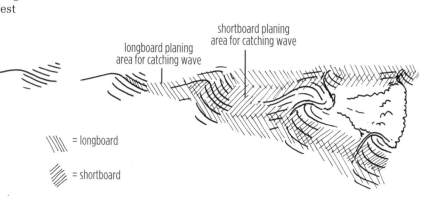

shortboard planing area for catching wave

longboard planing area for catching wave

$\big\backslash\big\backslash\big\backslash$ = longboard

$\big\backslash\big\backslash\big\backslash$ = shortboard

Speed. When it's time to paddle, paddle *hard*. Lily dipping is unlikely to yield desired results and is a one-way ticket over the falls. The faster you can paddle, the more waves you will catch.

You may notice that when you flatten your surfboard as you go from sitting to lying prone, the upward movement of the tail of the board provides a little jet propulsion, similar to the upward stroke of a dolphin tail. Use this extra boost in addition to your aggressive paddling when catching waves.

Angle. Usually, padding straight toward shore is best; however, sometimes you want to paddle in at a slight angle. A few wide paddle strokes can help you adjust the angle as needed.

For example, if the drop straight ahead is steep and you are at risk of pearling, you can angle your board in the direction that the wave is peeling instead of straight toward shore. Paddling at this angle also sets you up ahead of time to surf diagonally across the wave and eliminates the need for a bottom turn.

In contrast, if you are too far outside or over on the shoulder and you angle toward the shoulder (a), the drop may not be steep enough to allow you to start planing and catch the wave. Instead, angle your board toward the peak and down the steepest part of the wave (b) so your board planes as soon as possible. If the wave is approaching the shore at an angle or forming a bowl, the steepest part will be slightly toward the peak and not straight toward shore. Make sure the wave isn't too steep in this direction to make the drop. After you catch the wave and **fade**, or ride, toward the peak, you will need to do a bottom turn (c) in the direction that the wave is peeling so you are not on a collision course with the lip.

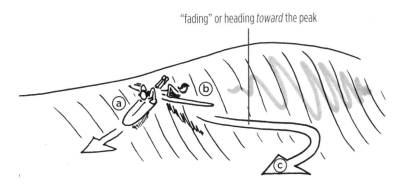

"fading" or heading *toward* the peak

Surf etiquette and safety reminder. You have to be aware of your surroundings (left, right, and ahead) to make sure that ① you still want to catch this particular wave, ② no one else has priority, ③ you are paddling in at the right speed and angle, and ④ no one is in your way.

With surfing, the choices are pull out (red light: the wave isn't suitable, or someone else has priority), keep watching and paddling but don't stand up (yellow light: it's unclear whether the person who has priority is going to make it past a section), or stand up (green light: the wave is yours if you want it). You may not know what choice to make until the last second, if that. If you are not sure, it is better to pass on a wave than drop in on someone else.

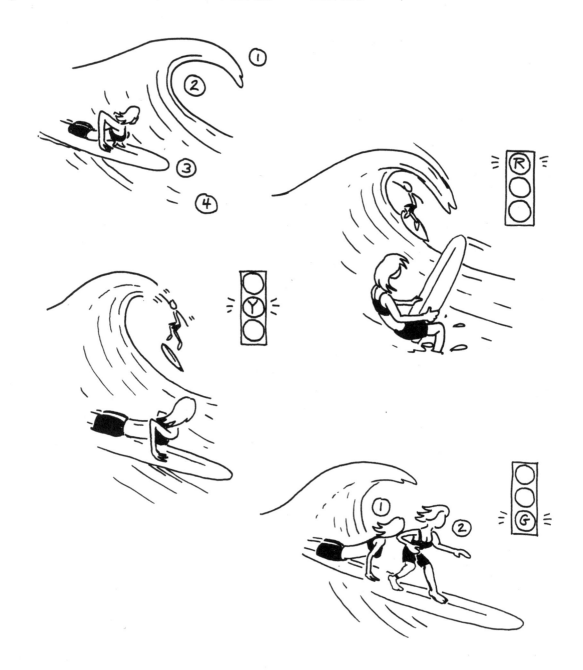

Backing off on a wave. If you take a second look and realize that this isn't a wave you want to catch, or it is already breaking, or someone else is on the wave or in your way, you can still back off. To put on the brakes, sit up, scoot your weight back, and drop both feet down into the sea anchor position. If the wave has already started to break, sit up and hunch forward to minimize the blow. If you feel you are at risk for being pitched over the falls, consider sliding off the board and holding onto it. Sometimes holding your board on edge (sideways to the lip) will reduce the board's profile.

Riding and Maneuvering

"Stand tall and fall, or stay low and go."
—Ed Guzman, Club Ed Surf School and Camps

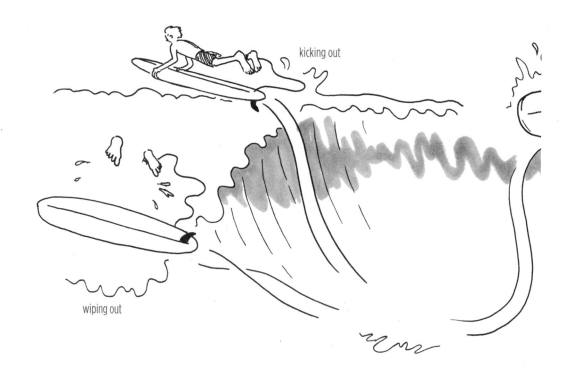

kicking out

wiping out

popping up

turning

controlling speed

STANDING UP ON WAVES

A ridiculously small portion of the time spent pursuing the sport of surfing is actually spent riding waves. Remarkably, the pleasure of these few minutes or seconds on a wave is totally worth hours of effort and expenditure.

Learning to surf is inherently challenging, but the overall experience should still be fun. If the fun factor isn't there for you and you are having a frustration session, mix things up a bit. Head over to a different peak, swap surfboards with your friend, paddle outside and soak up the sun, or just take a break.

You should have been practicing popping up on the living room rug and at the beach and visualizing proper form from Chapter 3 and the flip chart animation in the margins of this book. If you stand up and your feet aren't exactly where you want them, make a quick adjustment. Look forward and keep your knees bent to keep your butt low and your weight low and centered.

Psychology of Standing Up and Making the Drop

Making the drop is where the mental game of surfing comes in. If you think you are going to wipe out, you probably will. Once you give yourself a green light to drop in on a wave, you have to fully commit to making the drop. Any hesitation at this point is a one-way ticket over the falls. Visualize yourself making the drop and having a great ride. You will surprise yourself! As Yoda says, "Do or do not. There is no try."

Timing for Standing Up

The opportunity to catch a wave and stand up comes earlier on a longboard than on a shortboard.

"Premature e-standulation." —Ed Guzman

Timing for standing up on a green wave.

Experienced surfers pop up into a standing position as soon as their surfboards start planing, while beginners may stand up before the wave is steep enough to plane (premature e-standulation) and promptly sink ignominiously into the depths.

The trick is to take three more strokes after you *think* you have caught the wave, then pop up just as your board starts to drop beneath you and before you reach the bottom of the wave.

Other beginners are paralyzed on their bellies and try to stand up only at the end of the ride.

Pop up as soon as your board starts to drop out beneath you.

To better understand, try this experiment the next time you are alone in an elevator. While you are going up, lie on the floor ① and do a pop-up just as the elevator comes to a stop ②. The sensation of the elevator floor dropping out beneath you is how your surfboard feels when it is dropping down a wave. Use this moment of weightlessness on the elevator and the new space between your body and the floor to slide your feet beneath you. On a wave your body stays at the same height while the board drops down below and your feet fit in between.

To understand why you don't want to wait too long to stand up, try to pop up when the downward elevator stops ③. The increased g-forces that compress you into the floor (yechh) and make popping up difficult are similar to those you feel when you try to stand up at the bottom of a wave ④.

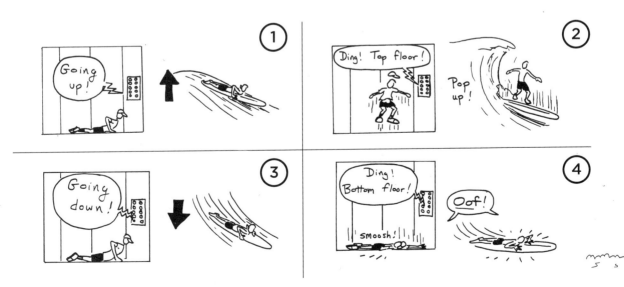

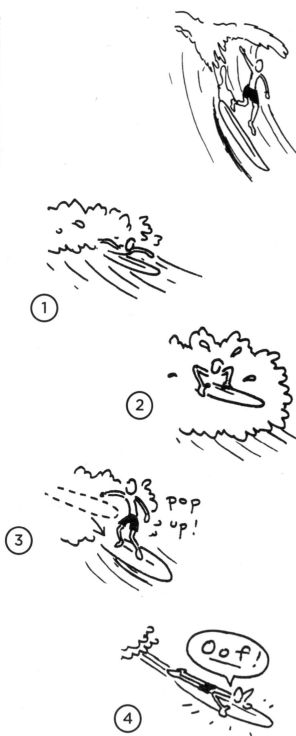

Timing for standing up on a breaking wave (late takeoffs). Late takeoffs are when you stand up just as the wave is breaking. Muscle memory (from popping up on the living room rug and on the beach), confidence, and commitment are key for landing the drop. You don't have to worry about paddling forward anymore (there isn't any time), so pop up as soon as possible (ignore the whitewater cascading around you). You may also want to pop up with your feet farther back to avoid pearling.

Timing for standing up in the soup (late, late takeoffs). Taking off in the **soup** is catching the foam from a wave that has already broken; it is not limited to beginners learning to stand up. While less stylish than taking off on a green wave, this extremely practical skill allows you to salvage situations where your position, timing, and/or judgment were off.

Surfers use this when the wave breaks outside of them but there is still a green shoulder they want to ride. ①Paddle straight in to generate some speed and ② hold on to your board tightly as the foam overtakes you. ③ Pop up as soon as the initial shock wave stops and you feel your board dropping down the foam pile. ④You can also hold on tight and wait to stand up until the foam spits you out onto the flats. While your board will be more stable away from the foam pile, you will be fighting gravity initially (like trying to stand up when a downward elevator stops) and missing valuable surfing time on the wave face. Staying on your belly until these g-forces are gone ⑤ is certainly an option, but the longer you wait, chances are that the best parts of the wave will be gone, too. If you choose not to stand up at all, just enjoy the belly ride in to shore.

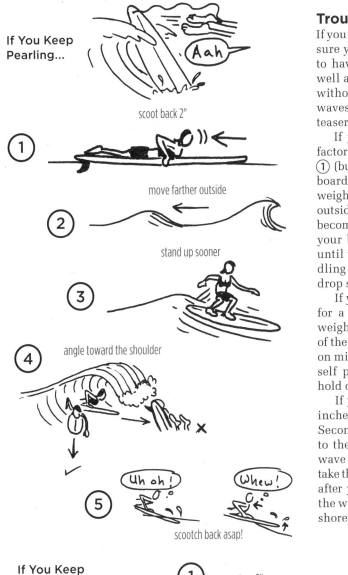

If You Keep Pearling...

Aah

scoot back 2"

①

move farther outside

②

stand up sooner

③

angle toward the shoulder

④

Uh oh! *Whew!*

⑤

scootch back asap!

Troubleshooting Catching Waves

If you are having trouble catching waves, make sure you are properly balanced on your board to have the speed needed to catch waves as well as a reasonable chance to make the drop without pearling. Also keep learning to read waves accurately to avoid both dumpers and teasers.

If you keep pearling, there are four basic factors to adjust. First, scoot two inches back ① (but not so far back that you slow down your board). You can also try popping up with your weight farther back. Second, paddle farther outside ② to catch the wave sooner before it becomes too steep. Third, stand up as soon as your board starts planing instead of waiting until the wave is too steep ③. Lastly, try paddling for waves at more of an angle so you don't drop straight down ④.

If you start to pearl when you are paddling for a wave, arch your back and scoot your weight back so the nose of the board pops out of the water ⑤; then stand up. This works only on minor miscalculations. If you do find yourself pearling and you haven't stood up yet, hold on to your board for a quicker recovery.

If you keep missing waves, first scoot two inches farther forward on your board ①. Second, move farther inside so you are closer to the glide zone and the steeper part of the wave ②. Third, paddle with more speed and take three more strokes (or two big breast strokes) after you are convinced that you have caught the wave ③. Fourth, try paddling straight into shore or slightly toward the peak ④.

If You Keep Missing Waves...

Darn it! I missed another one!

① scoot up 2"

② move closer in to shore

③ take 3 more strokes before you stand up

④ angle more toward the peak

WIPEOUTS

Wiping out is an integral part of surfing. Wipeouts usually happen when beginners are learning to stand up (thus the placement of this section), but even advanced surfers regularly wipe out (and quite spectacularly). Luckily, water is fairly soft, and surfers generally float, so the pummeling is transitory. If you don't wipe out frequently, you are not trying hard enough.

Assuming that you are unable to either kick out or sit down and stop, a controlled wipeout is the next best option. The main obstacles you are trying to avoid are your own surfboard, others surfers and their boards, and the bottom. Always try to control where your surfboard goes, and never shoot your board toward anyone else.

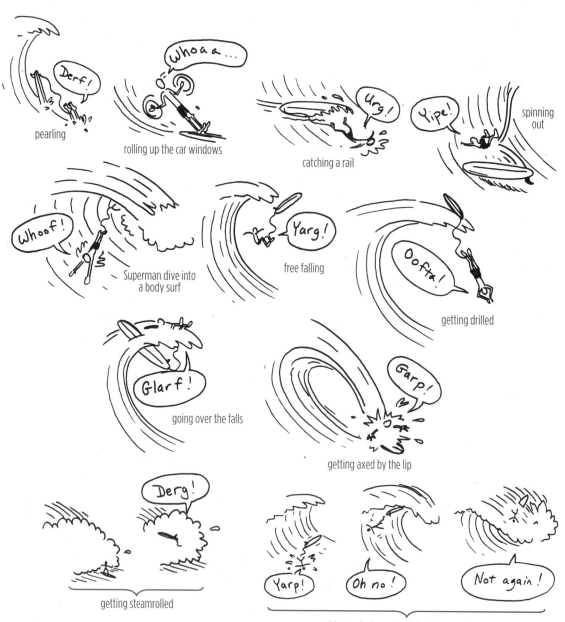

pearling

rolling up the car windows

catching a rail

Whoaa...

spinning out

Superman dive into a body surf

free falling

getting drilled

going over the falls

getting axed by the lip

getting steamrolled

getting sucked over the falls after your wipeout

try to hold on to your board
when you wipe out

If you can somehow safely grab hold of your surfboard as you fall, and can keep it from washing in with the wave, this will reduce your recovery time, and the surfers around you will appreciate it.

If grabbing your board is not a safe option, the best wipeout option on smaller waves is to do a starfish flop off the back of the board into the whitewater. The water is deeper in the foam pile, and you don't have to worry about your board hitting you. Never dive headfirst if you can avoid it. In places with shallow coral reefs, try to land flat with a belly flop or back flop.

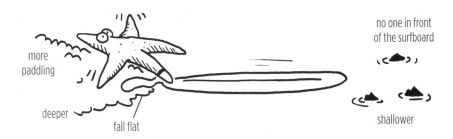

more
paddling

deeper

fall flat

no one in front
of the surfboard

shallower

Surfers who wipe out on large waves want to actually penetrate the wave face instead of skipping along the surface and risk being sucked over the falls.

getting sucked up over
the falls (really bad)

penetrating
(good if deep)

skipping (bad)

getting Maytagged

Being pummeled by a wave is similar to being a sock in a Maytag washer. Protect your head with your hands and arms, then relax and go with the flow. Most surfers have to hold their breath for only a few moments, but five seconds underwater can feel like five minutes. In some chaotic wipeouts you may exchange love taps with your surfboard, so hopefully you have a soft board or at least safety guards on its fins, nose, and tail.

If you do find yourself underwater for a prolonged period of time (say five seconds), relax and save your energy until the turbulence dies down and you can bob up.

relax and save energy while underwater

"tombstoning" surfboard

air & light ↑

dark & deep ↓

Tombstoning is when a surfboard surfaces but turbulence holds the surfer deep underwater like an anchor, so the surfboard points straight up like a tombstone. Open your eyes to reorient yourself to the surface, push up off the bottom, then swim up or climb your leash up to your surfboard.

After you wipe out, stay underwater for several seconds with your hands and arms protecting your head to make sure your surfboard doesn't nail you in the head when it springs back. Then surface (keeping your head covered), quickly climb back on your board, and take evasive maneuvers to avoid getting pummeled by the next wave.

stay underwater for a bit after you wipe out and cover your head as you come up

One of the side effects of wiping out is the insertion of massive amounts of sea water into your sinus passages. The trapped water will cascade out of your nostrils hours later at the most inopportune times (like that job interview).

RIDING WAVES

By now you should be a certified expert on wiping out. You should also have some experience in recognizing good beginner waves, paddling aggressively, and popping up on your feet at least some of the time. Once you are on your feet, the really hard part is over and you can start having fun. Don't worry about attempting any off-the-lip maneuvers at this point. Just start out as all surfers do, and ride straight toward shore. If your feet are not centered on the stringer or are too far forward or backward, you may have a second or two to shift your feet into proper position. Keep your knees bent and your body low. Remember to keep an eye out for other surfers around you.

feet centered on stringer

looking forward
body low
knees bent
nose up just a bit

riding straight toward shore

Steering or Turning

After you have some experience riding straight toward shore, the next thing to do is to steer your surfboard where you want to go. In general, you want to turn away from the breaking part of the wave and head toward the unbroken shoulder. Turning a surfboard is somewhat similar to turning a snowboard or skateboard in that you ① look and turn your shoulders in the direction you want to go, ② weight the board in the direction of the turn by pressing down with your toes or heels, and ③ shift your weight to the inside of the turn. At some point you will want to come out of the turn by ④ recentering your weight and looking at the next move.

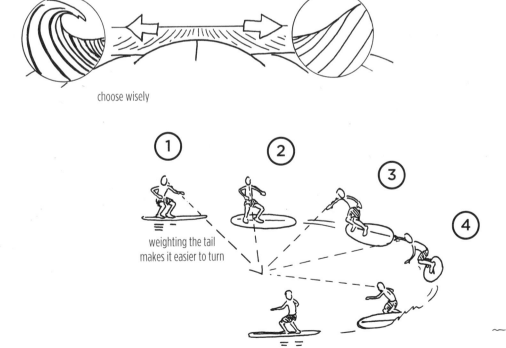

choose wisely

weighting the tail makes it easier to turn

Types of turns. The **bottom turn** is the initial turn that surfers make when they have dropped straight down the wave face and need to turn in the direction that the wave is peeling. This is the equivalent of the first hard turn that a roller coaster makes after the first big drop, and it's just as fun.

bottom turn

The **top turn** is the next turn that surfers make when they are angling up the wave face and need to turn back down to stay on the wave. Top turns can be made on the wave face (**roller coaster**; see page 149), at the wave crest (off-the-lip), or with the lip as a launching pad (aerial).

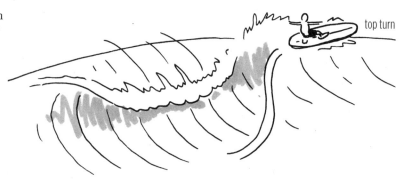

top turn

A **cutback** is a change of direction on the wave that turns you back in the direction you came from. Surfers use cutbacks if they race out ahead of the glide zone on the wave and need to turn back toward the curl. Once surfers complete a cutback and are heading back toward the breaking wave, they will have to turn once again in the direction the wave is peeling.

too far ahead of wave

cutback

turn toward shoulder again

Longboard turns vs. shortboard turns. The shorter a surfboard, the faster it can turn. **Longboard turns** are smooth and sweeping, while **shortboard turns** are quick and aggressive. You can shorten the effective length of a longboard by shifting your weight to the rear. With extra-large boards such as standup paddleboards, instead of keeping your rear foot centered on the stringer, you may actually have to shift it toward the rail you want to turn.

You can also adjust the relative looseness of your board (the ability of the tail to slide out) by adjusting the fin position, changing the fin type, and adding or removing fins (see Fins in Chapter 1).

looser turns ← → tighter turns

shortboard turns

longboard with weight shifted back

classic longboard turns

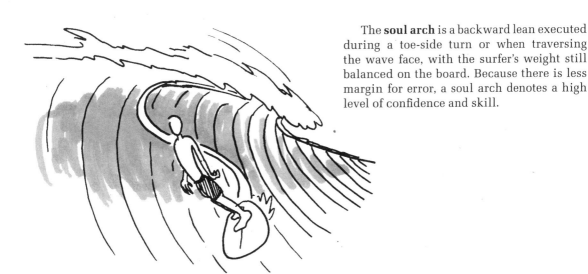

The **soul arch** is a backward lean executed during a toe-side turn or when traversing the wave face, with the surfer's weight still balanced on the board. Because there is less margin for error, a soul arch denotes a high level of confidence and skill.

The drop-knee turn. The drop-knee turn is an old-school technique required to turn the massive longboards of yesteryear to your heel side for a backside bottom turn or a frontside cutback. Instead of keeping your rear foot centered across the stringer and weighting your heel to turn the board as in a normal turn, move your rear foot toward the tail of the board and between the stringer and the backside rail. Angle your foot so it is parallel with the stringer and lower your stance so that only the ball and toes of your rear foot in contact with the deck. The weight on the tail and the rail help turn the surfboard. Although this method is no longer necessary with today's lighter and more maneuverable boards, it is still functional and stylish. Detailed descriptions of drop-knee turns for surfboards and skateboards can be found at http://www.surfacemotion.com.

Ideally, with all these turns, your surfboard and your body will be turning in the same arc at the same time. If you find yourself falling to the inside of the turn (common when first learning to turn a longer board), keep yourself centered until your surfboard actually turns underneath you, or shift your weight back so the surfboard turns faster underneath you. If you find yourself falling off to the outside of the turn (common when switching to a shorter board), bend your knees more and shift your weight more into the turn next time.

weight centered over turn

falling on *inside* of turn (weight may be too far forward)

falling on *outside* of turn

Angling and Trimming

Once you are comfortable standing up and surfing straight toward shore, you will want to experiment **angling** across an unbroken wave face. If you turn so you are facing the wave, you are riding frontside. If your back is to the wave, you are riding backside. It is generally easier to surf frontside than backside, but becoming proficient on both sides should not be difficult.

Angling is simply pointing your surfboard diagonally across the wave face. If you choose the right wave and direction, the glide zone will keep forming just ahead of your board, dramatically lengthening your ride. The easiest way to angle is simply to start out with your board pointed at that angle as you paddle for the wave. If you start surfing straight toward shore or toward the peak, you will want to do a bottom turn to start angling across the face.

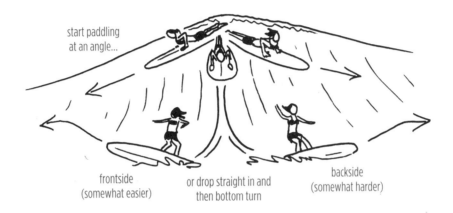

start paddling at an angle...

frontside (somewhat easier)

or drop straight in and then bottom turn

backside (somewhat harder)

Trimming is fine-tuning your board's position and balance for the best continuous glide down the line. Trimming is like finding that cat track on the ski hill that takes you all the way around the mountain at the perfect grade, or a mountain bike single-track trail at the perfect pitch that you can coast the whole way along a hillside. Staying in trim can be tricky if the shape of the wave changes and the glide zone moves around too quickly to follow. If you trim too high, you will go up and over the back of the wave; if you trim too low, the whitewater will catch up with you. Use subtle top and bottom turns to stay in trim and adjust your speed as needed (see next page).

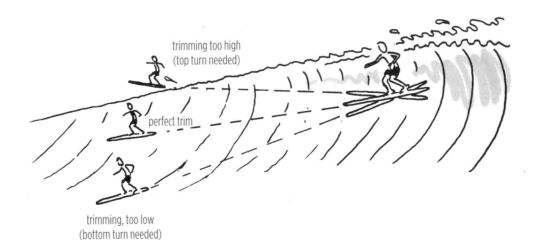

trimming too high (top turn needed)

perfect trim

trimming, too low (bottom turn needed)

Controlling Your Speed

Controlling your speed is a critical component for managing your progress along a wave, staying in trim, and executing different surfing maneuvers. There are several ways to control your speed.

First, you can steer your surfboard onto the faster or slower parts of a wave. Just as on a ski hill or in a skateboard park, steeper means faster. Surfers build speed by dropping down or cutting across the vertical peaks and walls. The flats in front of a wave and the low slopes on the shoulder are slower parts where surfers lose momentum.

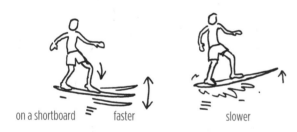

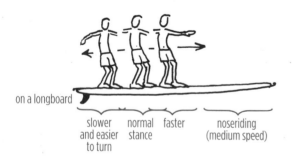

Second, you can control your overall progress down a wave with cutbacks and other turns. A **fade** is angling toward the curl when you drop in.

Third, adjust your speed by simply shifting your weight on the board. In general, the farther back you place your weight, the deeper the tail sinks, the more resistance you create, and more the board stalls. In contrast, weighting your forward foot accelerates the board (up to a point; then you pearl). Think of how weighting the front foot of a snowboard makes you go faster downhill. On your surfboard, start by adjusting your speed with your weight, and then combine this strategy with positioning your board on the wave.

Because shortboards are more sensitive to shifts in weight, a surfer on a shortboard can control the board's speed from one central stance. To slow down, shortboarders simply shift their weight toward their rear foot. To speed up, they pump their boards with their front foot to accelerate through flatter sections of waves.

Although it is possible to control a longboard's speed from one central stance, you can best speed up or slow down by walking up or down the board (see cross-stepping, next).

Fourth, a more advanced technique is using your body to stall or slow yourself down by projecting your hand, arm, or backside into a wave.

Cross-stepping. Cross-stepping up or down the length of a longboard is the best way to control its speed and turning ability and is an integral part of the style and pleasure of longboarding.

The Evolution of Cross-Stepping

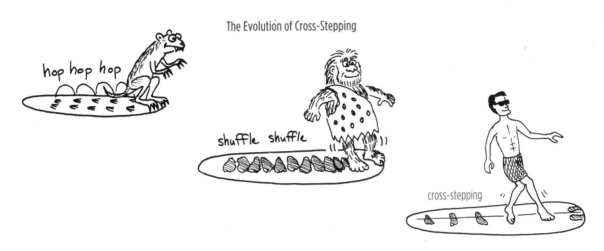

hop hop hop

shuffle shuffle

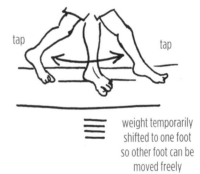

cross-stepping

Instead of hopping or shuffling up and down the board, experienced longboarders cross-step up and down the board. This motion is much smoother and faster. The trick is to be comfortable balancing temporarily on one foot so your other foot can move in front of or behind as needed.

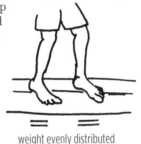

weight evenly distributed

tap

tap

weight temporarily shifted to one foot so other foot can be moved freely

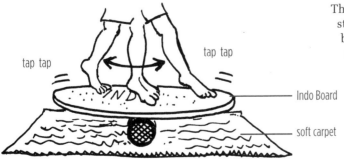

tap tap

tap tap

— Indo Board

— soft carpet

The best way to learn how to cross-step is on dry land with a balance board such as an Indo Board (check out Indoboard.com). Indo Board has an excellent video with this and other tips. For tips on using a skateboard to cross train for longboarding, check out Keith Johnson's website, http://www.surfacemotion.com.

To start, position front foot (A) and rear foot (B) at a diagonal surfing stance instead of in normal walking position. To move forward, ① start with your weight balanced between both feet; and press your thighs close together. ② Shift your weight forward until all of your weight is balanced on your front foot (A) ③, then move your unweighted rear foot (B) any distance in front of your front foot. ④ Place the ball of foot B down first, keeping this foot at the same angle across the stringer (if this feels a bit awkward, it should). ⑤ Keep shifting your weight forward so it is first evenly spread between both feet, and continue ⑥ until all your weight is entirely supported by foot B. ⑦ Bring foot A forward into a standard surfing stance (this will feel much more normal) and center your weight between both feet. ⑧ ⑨ Several sequences will be required to walk up to the nose of the board.

To walk backward, start by shifting your weight backward to your normal rear foot (B) and unweight your front foot (A). Tuck the knee of your front leg behind your rear leg and place the ball of foot A behind foot B. Shift your weight backward evenly between your two feet and then farther back so all your weight is on foot B. Next swing foot A in place behind foot B and distribute your weight normally between your two feet.

To practice on your board, take one step forward or backward at a time and then return to your normal stance. Next try two steps forward and backward and so on (this returns you to your normal stance).

Some longboard leashes attach around the calf instead of the ankle to reduce the chances of tripping while you are walking up and down the board. If your leash happens to become wrapped around or underneath a foot, a quick leg shake should be sufficient to disentangle yourself.

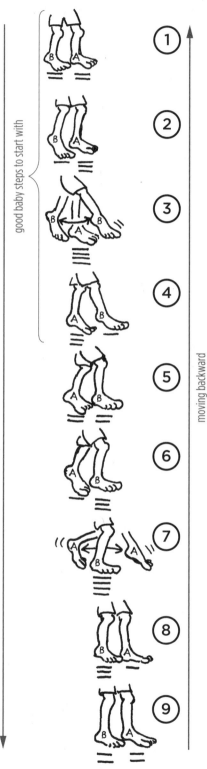

good baby steps to start with

moving forward

moving backward

normal stance

Evasive Maneuvers

When you are riding a wave, the main obstacles you are trying to navigate around are other surfers and sections of breaking waves. If you can't make it around a particular obstacle, your options are to kick out (page 158), straighten out (page 158), or wipe out (page 136).

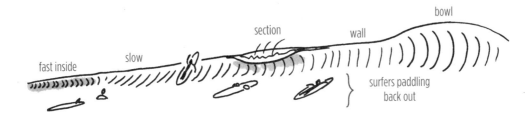

fast inside   slow   section   wall   bowl   surfers paddling back out

Avoiding other surfers. Ideally, all the other surfers will be paddling wide around the break or toward the whitewater to avoid getting in your way. At some point, however, you will have to maneuver around other surfers who are inside of you. Try to read the other surfers' intentions so you know which way they are paddling. If you are absolutely sure there is enough space, you can take the high line between the other surfer and the wave crest. If there is not enough space, either kick out over the back of the wave or go between the other surfer and the shore and try to regain the wave if possible. In crowded lineups, you may have to weave your way among several other surfers. Do not run anyone over!

kicking out

going between the other surfer and the lip

straightening out (or wiping out)

going between the other surfer and the shore

Making it around a section of whitewater. Waves often break in sections, with certain segments peeling at different speeds. Although going as fast as you can is the best way to make a section of wave, here are some other techniques that will help you navigate around, over, or through difficult sections of the wave.

Sometimes a section of whitewater will break just ahead of you, but it may still be possible to outrace the whitewater and regain the shoulder. First, gain as much speed as you can across the open face. If you have enough speed, you can carve out and around the whitewater in a long bottom turn.

making it around a section of whitewater with a bottom turn

If the whitewater catches up with you during your traverse, it will try to push the surfboard out from under you.

To stay on top of your board, keep your angle, squat down, and hold on to the shoreward edge of the board. If the wave isn't breaking top to bottom and you still have a green slope at the base of the whitewater, **pumping** the surfboard by weighting your front foot can add some speed.

Making it over a section of whitewater: A **floater** (see page 149) is used to go up, over, and around a section of whitewater that is breaking in front of you. Surfers need to read the wave well enough to anticipate the impending section and have enough time to position their boards. Climb up the wave face to the lip just before the section collapses, as you would for a **kickout** (see page 158). Instead of continuing over the back of the wave, turn your board parallel with the wave so the board projects on top of the whitewater. Then turn the board toward the shore and ride the falling whitewater down, keeping your knees bent.

Making it underneath a section of whitewater: In addition to being one of the best sensations in life, **tube riding** is an important skill for making it through a section of whitewater that is curling overhead.

Making it through the flat sections. Sometimes a wave will hit a deepwater trough and then back down or flatten out until it reaches shallow water again. To make it through this flat section, longboarders should lower their center of gravity, while shortboarders have to pump their boards to keep up. If crouching down isn't working and you start to lose the wave, lie back down and paddle hard to keep up with the wave. Stand back up as the wave picks up again.

whitewater blasting board out from under you

weight low

grab shoreside rail to help stabilize board

making it over a section of whitewater with a floater

making it underneath a section of whitewater with a tube ride

making it through a flat section by laying back down and paddling

Surfing Maneuvers

For most surfing maneuvers, surfers use the wave's energy to amplify their own actions. For example, a steep wave face is used like a skateboard ramp to build speed. Walls can be used as a half-pipe for carving turns. The wave crest, or **lip**, can be used as a catapult or ramp for aerial maneuvers. The foam pile can be used as a trampoline to accentuate turns or as a landing pad for aerials. All these maneuvers require the surfer to anticipate these wave features and be in the right spot at the right time.

Roller coaster. The roller coaster is a sequence of bottom turns and top turns, creating an up-and-down roller-coaster ride across the wave face. Indulge your inner grommet on the way to the beach and practice this maneuver by sticking your hand out the car window.

Roundhouse cutback. A round-house cutback is a high-speed cutback in the shape of a figure eight, with the second turn completed by climbing up and rebounding off the whitewater.

Off-the-lip. An **off-the-lip, snap, reentry**, or **off-the-top** is a top turn made at the crest of a wave. Your first introduction to an off-the-lip or cutback will be from grommets who shower you with their spray as they zip past.

Floater. A floater is used to go up, over, and around a section of whitewater that is breaking in front of you. Floaters are also a fun way to end a ride if the entire wave closes out.

Noseriding. Noseriding is the second-best sensation in surfing. See details on page 152.

Tube riding. Tube riding is the best sensation in surfing. See details on page 155.

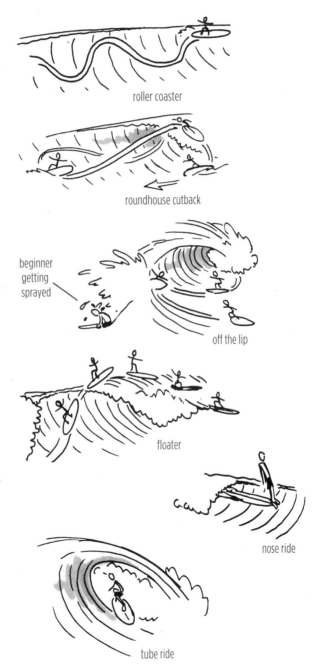

roller coaster

roundhouse cutback

beginner getting sprayed

off the lip

floater

nose ride

tube ride

Fun Tricks to Try

Surfboard tricks aren't just for experts. There are some fun basic tricks that beginners can work on that improve balance and wave-riding skills.

The sit and surf.

The sit and surf is a goofy, fun maneuver (also known as butt surfing) in which you use your hands to lower yourself from a standing position to a sitting position with your feet in front of you, like sitting in a kayak. Next, you bend your knees and spread your legs, then drop your lower legs in the water, which will flip you back into a normal paddling position. Then you extend your legs behind you, assume a prone position, and stand up again.

Spinner. A spinner is a 360-degree spin with your body while riding forward (leashes complicate this trick).

Switch stance. A useful skill, a switch stance is riding with either foot forward so you can always be riding frontside, no matter which direction the wave is breaking. Some surfers switch stance in mid-ride.

Head dip. A head dip is small-wave gesture that involves tucking and dipping your head down into the foam while riding frontside. Head dips are similar to tube rides except the tube may be too small for you to fit completely inside, or the tube is not well formed.

Headstand. A headstand on a surfboard is another trick for folks proficient in a headstand on dry land.

Coffin. The coffin is performed while lying on your back with your arms crossed and head back on the deck.

More Surfing Maneuvers and Tricks

These moves are beyond the scope of this book, but if you see folks doing them, you'll know what they are.

Fin-first takeoff. A fin-first takeoff involves lying backward, or fin first, on your surfboard, catching a wave, standing up, and then staying balanced   while your board fin catches the water and spins the board back around. Quick cross-stepping can be helpful here.

Helicopter. A helicopter or nose 360 is a flat-spinning move performed with the nose of the surfboard in the green water and the tail in the whitewater. The surfer plants an arm in the wave face and the fins break free of the whitewater, spinning the tail toward shore—similar to a fin-first takeoff. The surfer takes cross-steps to keep upright while the board spins nose first again.

360. A 360 is a dynamic spin where the surfboard stays in contact with the wave face or foam pile.

Barrel roll. A bodyboarding trick, a barrel roll involves riding your board up the wave face, going inverted under the lip, and landing upright to continue your ride.

Aerial. An aerial is when a surfer launches off the lip and catches air with the surfboard, sometimes spinning or inverting in the process.

Noseriding

Although not as dynamic or spectacular as other surfing maneuvers, noseriding is an art form unto itself. In this longboard-specific maneuver, the surfer cross-steps to the front quarter of the board and balances there for any length of time.

Although noserides may last only a few seconds, the sensation is remarkably satisfying. Imagine barefoot waterskiing without a boat or a towline. It's kind of like that.

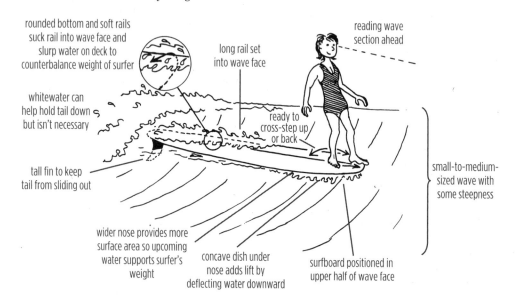

rounded bottom and soft rails suck rail into wave face and slurp water on deck to counterbalance weight of surfer

long rail set into wave face

reading wave section ahead

whitewater can help hold tail down but isn't necessary

ready to cross-step up or back

tall fin to keep tail from sliding out

small-to-medium-sized wave with some steepness

wider nose provides more surface area so upcoming water supports surfer's weight

concave dish under nose adds lift by deflecting water downward

surfboard positioned in upper half of wave face

The physics of noseriding. Being able to perch on the tip of a longboard appears to contradict basic physics, particularly to beginners who find themselves pearling constantly. The trick is setting the rail and tail into the top part of the wave so water is slurped across the tail to counterbalance the weight of the surfer on the nose.

Noseriding is best attempted on knee- to chest-high waves that peel consistently. Depending on the characteristics of your longboard, noseriding is possible in the pocket, along steep-walled waves, or out on the flatter shoulder of a wave. The rounded rails of a good noseriding longboard sweep water up and around the rear deck, anchoring the tail down. The surfboard's wide nose intercepts water coming up the wave face and helps produce lift in flatter sections of a wave. The straight rail of the surfboard provides the needed surface area for the rails to work their hydrodynamic magic, and the length of the board provides the needed leverage. For an in-depth description of the physics involved, check out http://www.tomwegenersurfboards.com/html/suction.html.

Setting up for a noseride. There are several ways to set your rail for a noseride. The challenge is that you can't see whether or not the rear of the surfboard is secure, so you have to develop a feel for it.

One option is to catch a wave at an angle and trim your surfboard in the upper half of the wave. It may take a few seconds for the rail to feel "set" into the wave.

Because pearling from an unsuccessful noseride can shoot your surfboard sky-high, hold on to the rail of your surfboard if you start to submerge so your board stays with you.

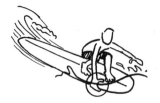

Another option is to start with a bottom turn and climb back up the face. Walk to the nose while the board is still climbing slightly up the wave face. Your forward motion helps fine-tune the surfboard into a proper trim position.

If you are trimmed too low on the wave, momentarily shift your weight back in a **kick stall** or **tail stand** (the surfing equivalent of a wheelie) to bring your board into proper position at the top of the wave face.

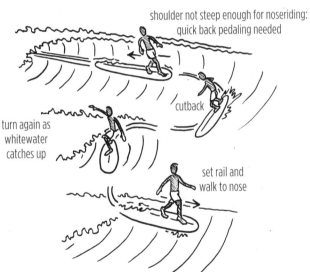

shift weight forward again

stalled board moves up wave face

once rail "feels" set, walk to nose

trimmed too low on wave face for a nose ride

shift weight back in a kick stall

shoulder not steep enough for noseriding: quick back pedaling needed

cutback

turn again as whitewater catches up

set rail and walk to nose

As long as the wave remains at the correct slope to anchor the tail with its hydrodynamic slurping action and the surfboard remains at the top part of the wave, a noseride is possible. The problem is that the peeling wave and the skimming surfboard don't always stay at the same speed. If the surfboard outraces the wave, the proper nose lift and tail suction will no longer be there and the surfer must cross-step back to remain upright. Surfers usually execute a cutback to bring themselves back toward the curl, and then turn again to go with the peeling wave and set themselves up for another noseride.

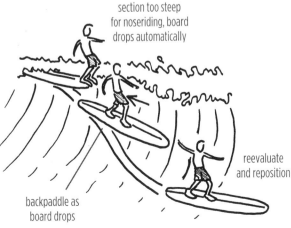

section too steep for noseriding, board drops automatically

If the wave outraces the surfboard and starts to break, the board will drop into the flats, and the surfer again will have to back-pedal promptly to remain upright. From here, surfers try to bottom-turn around the whitewater, and try to catch up with the green wave again (see Evasive Maneuvers on page 147).

backpaddle as board drops

reevaluate and reposition

Noseriding maneuvers. Noseriding is all about reading a wave and taking advantage of noseriding opportunities, no matter how brief. When walking up to the nose, watch for any potential pearling. Be ready to backpedal at a moment's notice and then cross-step forward to the nose again. A good way to practice is simply to cross-step half a step forward and then, before too much can go wrong, cross-step back. Go a little farther each time.

Cheater five. A cheater five is a noseriding maneuver where you position one foot over the nose without fully committing all your weight to the nose. For this maneuver, crouch low and extend a foot to hang five toes over the nose while most of your weight is still back on your rear foot. The classic hanging five position is with five toes over the nose of the board and your weight on both feet. **Hanging ten**, which is placing all ten toes over the edge, requires more commitment and sensitivity. For the last step to hang ten, surfers shift their stance from a diagonal, snowboarding stance to a parallel, skiing stance. Some accomplished surfers can even perform this backward and hang heels (and beyond).

Cross-stepping forward and backward is an important component for successful noseriding, although most learners lapse back to some sort of shuffle or hop in moments of crisis.

cheater five

hanging five

hanging ten

hanging heels

Tube Riding

Tube riding (also known as clocking time in the green room or getting tubed, barreled, shacked, slotted, covered up, et cetera) is one of the best sensations in surfing and in life. It actually is worth all the hype. Imagine trying to outrace an avalanche, but then you deliberately slow down so the avalanche comes up and over you, and then you accelerate and emerge unscathed (some of the time). Wave selection, board placement, and controlling your speed are key to successful tube riding. Because shortboards are more maneuverable and compact than longboards, they are the best overall tool for tube riding.

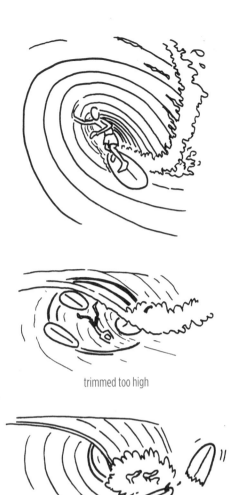

Setting up for a tube ride. You can't get tubed if the wave isn't barreling. Look for a wave that barrels and still leaves you enough time to possibly make it to the shoulder (if you care about that part). Once you've found a wave with a makeable tube, the key is to adjust your board's position and speed so the lip comes over you and covers you up, still leaving a slot of green water for you to ride on.

If you are trimmed too high, you will get sucked up and go over the falls. If you are positioned too low, you will get axed by the lip.

One option is to make a bottom turn and then position yourself under the lip. Another option is to take off at an angle and head directly into position. If the wave is peeling very quickly, simply go as fast as you can as the lip comes over you, and try to make it to the shoulder.

trimmed too high

trimmed too low

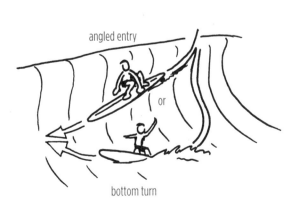

angled entry

or

bottom turn

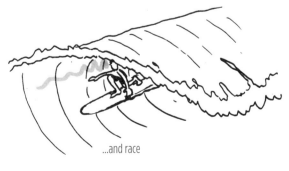

...and race

If the wave is breaking more slowly, you risk outracing the tube entirely and shooting out onto the shoulder (which would still be a fun ride). Surfers can deliberately stall by shifting their weight to the rear of the board or dragging an arm or their backside in the wave face to slow down.

Another option is to go in through the backdoor and take off behind the peak, tucking underneath the lip as it pitches over. On a spilling wave, the section ahead would close out, but if the wave forms a barrel you can make it through the interior of the wave.

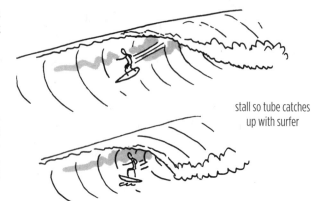

stall so tube catches up with surfer

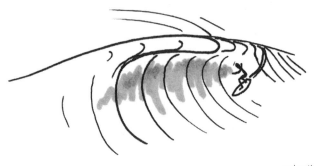

going through the backdoor

Tube-riding positions. In order to fit within the shifting confines of the tube and not be whacked in the head by the throwing lip, frontside surfers assume a tucked position. A standup barrel is when a phenomenally accomplished surfer casually stands upright in a phenomenally large barrel.

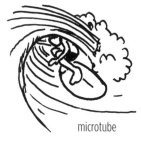

microtube

standup barrel

Backside surfers may grab their outside rail with their shore-side hand, lying forward and dragging their wave-side hand in the wave face (also known as a pigdog stance).

Backside tube riders can also use a layback stance, skimming their rear arm, back, and bottom in the wave face to slow their speed down so the lip overtakes them.

The best way to end a tube ride is to make it out of the tube to the shoulder.

If the wave is closing out in front of you, look to see if you can still make it out of the tube and straighten out in front of the whitewater, and thus avoid getting guillotined by the lip or going over the falls. Ducking under this falling curtain and into the flats is known as escaping through the doggie door.

When you are trapped by a closeout tube, the best strategy is to either dive off the front of the board or fall off the back, protecting your head in either case. Expert surfers avoid going over the falls by submerging through the wall of the tubing wave with their boards.

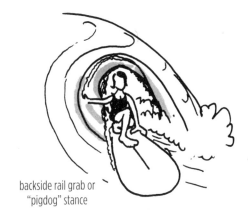

backside rail grab or "pigdog" stance

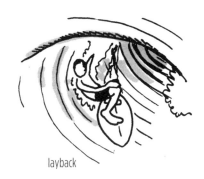

layback

Woo hoo!

escaping to the shoulder

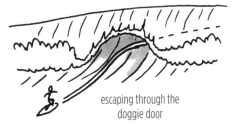

escaping through the doggie door

Ending Your Ride Gracefully

Aside from wiping out (which you will soon be quite proficient in), there are four ways to end your ride under your own terms: **kicking out**, **stalling**, **bailing**, and **proning out**. Before you end your ride, take a look over your shoulder to see what the wave behind you is doing. If a large set wave is coming, you may want to ride farther away from the impact zone before you end your ride.

Kicking out (also known as **pulling out**). Kicking out is a sharp turn up and over the wave face to exit a wave. Surfers kick out if they have inadvertently dropped in on someone, if the wave is about to close out, or if the wave is dying. Kicking out is preferable to wiping out or stalling out because you are already on the backside of the wave and have your board in hand, ready to paddle back out.

To execute a kickout, turn up the wave face while weighting the tail of the board so the wave leaves you behind. As you pass over the crest into the wave trough behind, reach down to grab both rails and then lie down so you can resume paddling as soon as you land on the backside of the wave. If you have a lot of speed when you kick out, you may fly out of control. Flying kickouts are kind of fun if you don't land on your board or someone else.

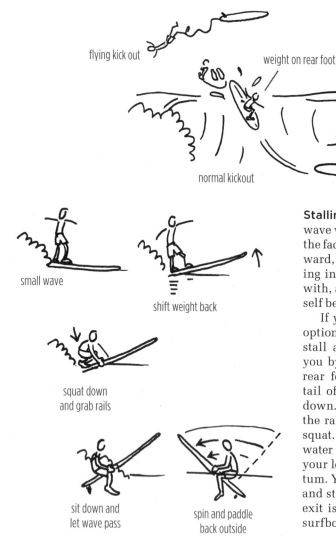

flying kick out

weight on rear foot

normal kickout

small wave

shift weight back

squat down
and grab rails

sit down and
let wave pass

spin and paddle
back outside

Stalling, squatting, and sitting. Often the wave will close out before you are able to climb the face and kick out. You are now surfing shoreward, trapped by the whitewater. Although riding in the whitewater is good practice to start with, at some point you will want to stop yourself before you hit the beach.

If you are unable to kick out, the next best option for ending a ride on a small wave is to stall and sit down so the whitewater passes you by. While you are riding in, weight your rear foot, or cross-step back to the tail. The tail of your surfboard will sink, slowing you down. At the same time, reach down and grab the rails of the board, and lower yourself to a squat. If the wave is small enough, the whitewater should pass you by. Sit down and drop your legs over the side to stop all your momentum. You can now do a frog kick to spin around and start paddling back out. The benefit of this exit is that you are always in control of your surfboard.

Proning out. If the whitewater is particularly large and turbulent, surfers may ride farther inside past the impact zone until the wave dissipates somewhat. Because it can be hard to stay standing in the whitewater, many surfers lie back down and prone out, or **belly-ride** the surfboard in. Squat down, grab the rails, and then lie down the board, scooting back a bit to keep the nose up. Hold on tight and then either sit up and stall or bail when you want to stop, or stand back up again on the re-form.

scoot back
a bit

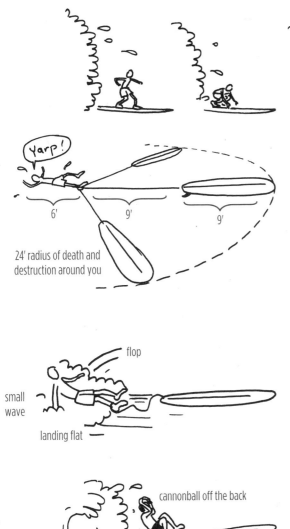

Yarp!

6'   9'   9'

24' radius of death and
destruction around you

flop

small
wave

landing flat

cannonball off the back

bigger wave

Bailing. If the whitewater is too big to gracefully exit by stalling out, another option is to **bail** by jumping off the back of your surfboard. It is important that the coast is clear in front of you. Many beginners simply fall off their board without looking ahead, shooting their board in all directions. If you have a 9-foot surfboard with a 9-foot leash and are 6 feet tall, this means that anyone within a 24-foot radius could get clobbered. If there are folks in front of you, either bail well before you reach them or wait until you have gone past them.

If the wave is small and the water is shallow, back flop into the whitewater. If the wave is big and the water is deep, a cannonball-style exit off the back of the board will help you penetrate the water so the whitewater passes over you. If you are riding along the face of the wave, you can sometimes bail by jumping over the back of the wave. This is similar to a kickout, but your board stays on the beach side of the wave to take the hit (and potentially hits others). With better wave judgment, timing, and board control, you will be able to kick out with your surfboard more often.

If a wave closes out and you aren't interested in riding the whitewater, it is generally better to bail earlier rather than later. The longer you surf toward shore, the shallower the water becomes, the longer the paddle back out will be and the more waves you will have to deal with.

belly/back flop
over the whitewater

GETTING BACK TO THE BEACH AFTER YOUR SESSION

It is always best to leave the surf while wanting more. Ideally, you catch a wave back to shore (see Chapters 4 and 5), but beware the infamous "one more wave" syndrome (which causes all surfable waves to disappear) and head back to the beach while you still have a few paddle strokes left in you and before you get too cold and tired. It is best to catch a decent wave into shore than to wait outside for the perfect wave until you are completely hypothermic and end up paddling in an hour later.

Be aware that access points may have changed since you first left the beach, and have a backup plan. If you plan well and catch a wave in, you will probably want to keep riding it past the point where it closes out. Because it can be hard to stay balanced upright in the whitewater, many surfers lie back down and prone out or belly-ride their board in. From here you can ride the whitewater the rest of the way in.

As described in Chapter 3, stop before you belly-ride all the way to the shore break by angling your board into the whitewater or by sitting up. As a last resort, flop backward off your board and into the whitewater before you reach the shore break. Time your exit through the shore break carefully (see page 98 in Chapter 3) and keep an eye on the ocean.

Once on shore, take a look back at the ocean to help calibrate your wave-judging gauge. Chances are the waves will look significantly smaller than when you were out there a few minutes ago. Also see if you were surfing in the best place for your abilities or if there is a different place you should try next time.

"It sure seemed a lot bigger when I was out there."

SURFING BENCHMARKS

Celebrate reaching these benchmarks and keep working toward those that you haven't yet accomplished. Not all these benchmarks are necessarily pleasurable, but they are noteworthy rites of passage.

Making it Outside

Turning Turtle

Catching Your First Belly Ride in the Soup

Wiping Out

Pearling

Going over the Falls

Standing Up!

Catching Your First Green Wave

Angling on Your Frontside

Angling on Your Backside

Kicking Out

Cutback

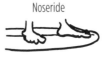

Catching a Wave as Tall as You Are

Cross-Stepping

Noseride

Getting Tubed (Even for a Millisecond)

Catching a Wave all the Way to the Beach (Remember to Stop before You Reach the Shore Break)

Post-Session Nasal Drip

Surfer's Swag: A Grab Bag of Information

A surf trip, or surfari, is an integral part of the surfing experience. Surf adventures are available for folks ranging from rank beginners to hardcore experts. Remember that there are no guarantees (the surf could be flat, too big, or blown out the whole week), but waves are only one part of the adventure. Don't forget to pack your sense of adventure and humor to make the most of your trip.

SURF SCHOOLS AND SURF CAMPS VS. TRAVELING ON YOUR OWN

Even if you are the do-it-yourself type who thinks that sports lessons (ski/snowboard/kayak) are for wimps, I highly recommend investing in a surf lesson or starting your adventure from a surf camp. Traveling on your own is also a perfectly reasonable option. You can base out of a central location if the surf break is within walking distance, or you can rent a car to tour around.

Surf Schools

Surf schools can be an excellent way to steepen your learning curve in a focused and supportive environment. If you are short on time and money, investing in even a two-hour session can be worthwhile. Each hour spent practicing in a quality surf lesson is equivalent to a full week of flailing on your own. Surf instructors should be able to take you to the best beginner breaks, set you up with a soft longboard that is less likely to hurt you or anyone else, provide critical tips, and help you progress much faster.

Surf Camps

Surf camps are hostels or resorts designed to cater to surfers and their needs. The camps are usually situated near an intermediate or advanced surf break and may have guides and boats for hire to

"Adventure is not in the guidebook and Beauty is not on the map.
Seek and ye shall find. "

—Terry and Renny Russell, *On the Loose*

take you to the best break working that day. These camps usually have a restaurant, a steady supply of beer, and surf magazines and videos to keep folks stoked between sessions.

Because surf camps often cater to experienced surfers, check to see if there are any beginner breaks nearby or if the camp provides beginner lessons. Most surfers coming to surf camps bring their own boards, so check ahead to make sure there are longboards to rent.

Instructional surf camps that cater to beginners are terrific options for improving your skills. A typical schedule in a surf camp is a hearty breakfast, a stretch session, an outdoor class using sand diagrams, a morning surf session, lunch, a nap, an afternoon surf session, a rest break, an evening surf session, and dinner.

Although many of these breaks were once uncrowded, surf camps have definitely popularized formerly remote areas, so don't expect to be the only one in the water. (Despite what the camp websites may say.)

Although surf camps are not cheap, you will save a lot of time by not searching for suitable waves on an unfamiliar coastline. You might be able to significantly lower the price if you camp out instead of staying in a room, moderate your beer intake, use public transportation to go to and from the airport, and attend in the off-season.

Boat Trips

Boat trips are a great way to access remote surf breaks. The trips may be offered as part of a surf camp experience or be open to any paying surfers. Keep an eye on the boat during your session in case the captain decides to move to another break. If the captain is going to drop you off, agree on a time for him to come back and pick you up. Bring plenty of sunscreen, drinking water, and snacks on the boat with you.

wide-brimmed sun hat

long sleeve rash guard

water

sunscreen

Questions to Ask

When looking for a surf school or surf camp, ask the following questions:

- For lessons, what is the student:instructor ratio? (You want at least one instructor per four students.) One on one is best.
- What type of equipment is available for rent? Do you have longboards? How long? (A 7'0" is not a longboard). If so, do you have soft or spongeboards (and not just soft-tops or fiberglass boards)?
- How long have the instructors been surfing? How long have they been teaching?
- Do all the instructors have current CPR/first aid/lifesaving certification?
- Does the surf school have a permit? (Many areas now require permits.)
- What are the surf conditions generally like this time of year?
- What is the probability of finding good conditions for beginners at this time of year? What are the local winds like?
- What is the water temperature? Are wetsuit rentals available?
- Are there nearby alternative breaks if the surf is too large or too small? Do you provide transportation (van or boat)? What is the cost?
- What nonsurfing activities (ping pong, pool, fishing, scuba diving, sea kayaking, bird-watching, whale watching, shopping, et cetera) are there in case the waves are too small/big or you want to take a rest day?
- Do you offer all-women, kids, or other specialty classes?
- Are they insured?

Bonuses can include the following, but be sure you ask how much they are so you don't end up with a surprise at the end of your week:

- Airport pickup and drop-off
- Video footage of yourself surfing, with critique from instructors
- Masseuse
- Yoga classes
- Quality food
- Lodging
- Hot tubs for soaking sore muscles
- Tour of a surfboard factory
- Nightlife (or quiet life)
- Clients with similar goals
- Security of valuables (available safe and/or lockers)
- Photographs of yourself surfing from the shore or in the water

When and Where to Go

Because there are surf camps on almost every surfable coastline around the world, you can find good conditions anytime of year. From Tofino, British Columbia, to Tamarindo, Costa Rica, there are hundreds of surf camps and surf schools to choose from. Start by researching on the Internet and then e-mail potential surf camps to find out more information.

As a beginning surfer, you don't need (or want) double-overhead waves, so you can learn to surf in what other surfers might consider marginal conditions, and even go in the shoulder (off) seasons when rates are cheaper. However, off seasons can be windy or totally flat, so check forecasting sites like surfline.com before booking.

Training and Preparing for Your Surf Trip

You will get the most out of your surf trip if you are physically prepared ahead of time.

Exercise. Even if you might think you are in good shape, when surfing you will use muscles you never knew you had. Still, you can greatly increase your learning curve, be safer in the water, and reduce your recovery time with some basic proactive measures.

First, exercise regularly before you go (starting three months, not three days, before you leave). The best exercise (next to surfing itself) is swimming. Plan on swimming for an hour three times a week right before your trip. For folks with shoulder or rotator cuff problems, visit your doctor and physical therapist to see what strengthening exercises you should be doing. A good way to practice basic balance is on an Indo Board (see page 145).

Flexibility is also important. Take a yoga class regularly and develop your own routine. An excellent book on specific training techniques is Rocky Snyder's *Fit to Surf*.

Chills and ills. Unfortunately, many warm-water destinations have all sorts of tropical diseases. Any number of maladies—from Montezuma's revenge to malaria and dengue fever to botflies—can ruin a vacation. Visit your local health clinic well ahead of time so you can get vaccinated and take other precautions. Where mosquitoes are a problem in the evenings, wear long-sleeved shirts, long pants, and socks treated with permethryn and dab deet on any exposed skin.

What to Bring

Although this may sound obvious, make sure you have guaranteed access to a surfboard that works for you.

Rent

Although most experienced surfers disdain renting, for beginning surfers it may be cheaper and easier to rent than carry your own board (particularly with airport fees). At the time of publication, surfboard rentals were $10 to $25 per day or $100 to $150 per week, although prices are usually much higher at popular resorts such as Waikiki. If you can, contact surf shops, surf schools, and surf camps ahead of time about rental selection and prices. Weeklong rentals can be cheaper than daily rentals.

Bringing Your Own

If you do decide to bring your own board, it is best to have one that does fairly well in a wide range of conditions. Call the airlines before buying tickets to find out the baggage fee for your surfboard round-trip. These fees can be exorbitant, so it is worthwhile to compare different airlines. When checking in at the airport, be prepared to pay, but do not remind them that there is a fee. There is a small chance that airline personnel may not charge you.

Because longboards are difficult to transport, an upcoming trip might be a good excuse to branch out and try a funboard, fish, or even a shortboard.

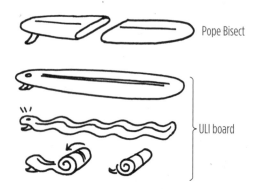

Pope Bisect

ULI board

Practice on your new board before you go! Two travel-friendly alternatives are the inflatable ULI board (http://www.uliboards.com) and the breakdown Pope Bisect (http://www.bisect.com).

Properly pack your surfboard in a travel case (see page 36) to minimize damage. Remove the fins or, if they are glassed in, pad them with towels or foam blocks. Secure pipe insulation along the rails, nose, and tail. You could also consider wrapping your sleeping bag or clothes around the board. Bring soft surf racks and straps to transport your board via taxi or rental car. Don't forget a travel ding-repair kit suitable for your board, a spare leash, a few bars of surf wax suitable for the local water temperature (the warmer the water, the harder the wax), and some surf stickers for the local grommets.

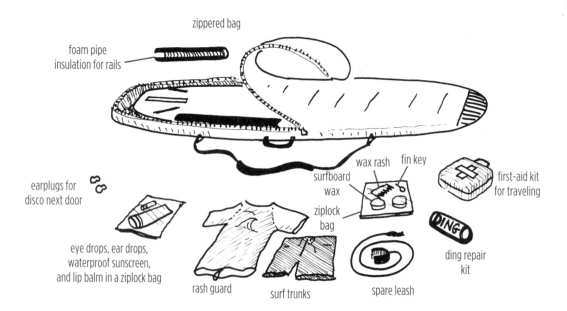

zippered bag

foam pipe insulation for rails

earplugs for disco next door

eye drops, ear drops, waterproof sunscreen, and lip balm in a ziplock bag

rash guard

surf trunks

surfboard wax

wax rash

fin key

ziplock bag

spare leash

ding repair kit

first-aid kit for traveling

SURF SAFETY TOPICS

Sunburn and Skin Cancer

Of all the surfing hazards—razor-sharp reefs, great white sharks, and swarms of jellyfish—the most probable and preventable injuries are from the sun. A bad sunburn on Day 1 can ruin a weeklong surf vacation in Costa Rica as well as increase your chances of skin cancer. Wear sunscreen all the time, and don't forget the backs of your knees, the tips of your ears, and a receding hairline. Be sure to apply sunscreen in the gap on the small of your back between your rash guard and swimsuit. Apply sunscreen 20 minutes before you hit the water, and reapply often. Also wear a long-sleeved rash guard with a sun protection factor (SPF) of 30 or greater. Wear a hat, long-sleeved shirt, and long pants when you aren't in the water and drink plenty of water to stay hydrated. Visit a dermatologist regularly to make sure your moles are behaving themselves.

Pterygium, or Surfer's Eye

Pterygium, or **surfer's eye,** is an unsightly growth of thick vascular tissue on the white of the eye caused by external irritation. Pterygia are common with outdoor activities wherever ultraviolet radiation, dust, salt, and wind can dry or irritate the eye. While eye surgery may be necessary to remove a pterygium that starts to occlude vision, the growth can be prevented or controlled by using lubricating eye drops frequently, wearing sunglasses at the beach, and wearing specialized surfing sunglasses in the water to block UV light (see Seaspecs, Barz, Oakley Waterjackets, Silverfish, or Kurtis Surf Goggles). Polarized glasses are best.

Cold-Water Surfing

Protect yourself from hypothermia by wearing as much neoprene as you need to, and head in to warm up **before** you start shivering.

Surfer's Ear and Swimmer's Ear

Surfer's ear is a common malady for surfers, kayakers, and divers who spend lots of time in cold water. Prolonged exposure to cold water results in bony ear growths that can seal your ear canal shut over time, requiring painful (and loud!) surgical drilling and/or chipping to remove. Surfers in cool and cold water should always wear earplugs to delay the onset of surfer's ear. Wearing a hood also helps.

If water stays trapped in your ear, painful ear infections or swimmer's ear can result. Help clear out any leftover water with a few drops of Swim Ear (or make your own using 50% distilled white vinegar and 50% isopropyl alcohol).

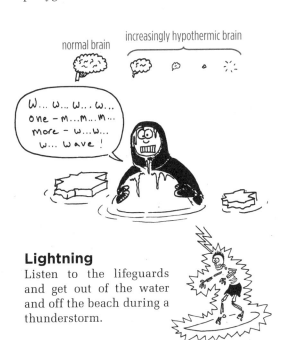

Lightning

Listen to the lifeguards and get out of the water and off the beach during a thunderstorm.

Sharks and Other Critters

Compared to the risks posed by talking on your cell phone on the way to the surf break and what your breakfast donut is currently doing to your arteries, sharks are the least of your worries. Sharks kill about ten people per year (most attacks are unfortunate cases of mistaken identity), while humans kill roughly 100 million sharks per year (wastefully and needlessly threatening ocean ecosystems).

Regardless of the odds, bobbing in the middle of the food chain is a humbling experience. Avoid needless risks such as surfing next to sea lion or seal colonies, sea turtle nesting grounds, murky rivermouths, and surfing alone. Check with locals about recent sightings and rivermouth breaks. Otherwise, don't worry about it.

Although stingrays, sea snakes, and stonefish are quite docile unless you aggravate them by stepping on them or picking them up, they have a highly potent venom. Seek immediate attention if stung or bitten by any of these marine critters. For stingray wounds, soak the site in hot water (as hot as the patient can tolerate without burning him) to help neutralize the venom and offer some pain relief. To avoid being stung by a stingray, shuffle your feet when wading through the shallows.

Jellyfish are obvious hazards, but so are their invisible larva. Swimmer's itch, sea bather's eruption, or sea lice (a misnomer) are commonly used to describe skin irritation from either jellyfish or crab larva. Swimmers may encounter large swarms of these creatures during certain times of

seaweed speed bump

If you find yourself and your surfboard tangled in seaweed or kelp, climb on your surfboard and start paddling. The strands of kelp will slide down to your leash. Once your leash goes taut, lift your ankle quickly while paddling forward and repeat until clear.

If you ride across kelp with your surfboard, your fin can snag, stopping your surfboard and leaving you flying through the air. Avoid kelp clumps or lower your stance and brace for a seaweed speed bump.

year. Anytime the larva become pinched between folds of skin (say in your armpit or groin area), they sting or pinch back. Frantic swimmers have been known to rip off their swimsuit on the beach in an effort to rid themselves of these wee beasties. Pay attention to swimming advisories and stay out of the water if there are swarms of those or hazardous jellyfish. Should you find yourself stung, wash any remaining stinging strands off with salt water. Peeing on the site doesn't help at all and fresh water only antagonizes the little buggers. Follow up with a vinegar rinse to help neutralize the venom.

Red tide refers to algae blooms that can result in large fish kills and make shellfish unsuitable for human consumption, but it does not affect surfers and swimmers.

Coral reefs form beautiful waves, but the animal architecture can be razor sharp and play havoc with bare skin. Use booties to protect your feet, avoid low tide, and land flat when wiping out to avoid getting raked across the coral (see Wiping Out in Chapter 6 on page 136). Consider using a helmet as well. Treat reef cuts as you would any wound and disinfect thoroughly.

Sea urchins present another prickly situation for surfers. As with coral, try not to hit the bottom. Remove any embedded spines and treat like any puncture wound.

CONSERVATION: GIVING SOMETHING BACK

After six chapters of telling folks how great the ocean is and how to enjoy it, I have to tell you the bad news: humans are screwing it up big-time. An astonishing number of surf breaks in the United States are contaminated with pollution from storm drains and sewer outfalls. In addition, more and more pristine coastlines and valuable wetlands are being lost to reckless development. Sea turtles, sharks, coral reefs, and valuable fisheries are all spiraling toward extinction. Luckily, there are a few simple things that caring folks like you can do to reverse these trends.

Start at Home

Even if you live hundreds of miles from the ocean, there is a stream or river near you on its way to the sea. Join your local conservation organization and learn how to protect your own watershed. Mark storm drains so no one dumps their motor oil there, conserve water in your household, and buy locally produced food when possible.

"Green" Up Your Lawn

Prevent chemicals from flushing downstream by reducing the amount of fertilizer and other chemicals you use. Save water by irrigating your lawn wisely (or xeriscaping!).

NO DUMPING
DRAINS TO RIVER

Don't Flick Your Butt

In addition to being harmful to your health, cigarettes are the most prevalent type of litter on Earth. Globally, more than 4 trillion cigarette butts end up as litter every year, with the majority of them washing through storm drains into our rivers and oceans. Although a cigarette butt is small, this number equates to more than 176 million pounds of litter annually in the United States. Because cigarette butts are actually made of plastic (the cotton-like fibers are actually cellulose acetate), each butt takes years to break down. In the meantime, seabirds and other animals can accidentally ingest them and die. Cigarette butts also contain toxic chemicals such as arsenic, formaldehyde, lead, and benzene, which can contaminate water and harm the critters at the base of the food chain.

Reduce Plastic Use

In addition to being energy intensive, plastic debris entangles thousands of animals every year. Even innocuous items such as balloons and their strings can harm birds and marine mammals that mistake them for food, so never release balloons into the sky. Cut plastic six-pack rings before throwing them away.

Reduce the need for plastic bags by buying reusable bags, and avoid buying bottled water (filtered tap water tastes great). While traveling overseas, use a portable filter or UV purifier to treat your water instead of buying endless plastic bottles. Practice the reuse, reduce, and recycle mantra for other things as well.

Eat Sustainably Harvested Seafood

Seafood can be a healthy part of your diet, so support sustainably managed fisheries such as wild Alaskan salmon and avoid unsustainable fisheries such as farmed Atlantic salmon and Chilean sea bass. Limit your intake of fish with high mercury levels. Print out a pocket guide to sustainable seafood from the Monterey Bay Aquarium's website at www.seafood-watch.org and make copies for your friends.

Clean Up Your River or Beach

Participate in a river or beach cleanup day or organize your own. Contact your local conservation group to learn how.

Join the Surfrider Foundation

Organizations such as the Surfrider Foundation are fighting back to stop pollution at its source and protect coastlines for both beachgoers and fish. Support their work by becoming a member (a percentage of the proceeds from this book are donated to Surfrider).

Educate Yourself and Make Yourself Heard

There is a lot of misinformation out there on conservation issues. Educate yourself, attend public meetings, and write letters to local elected officials and the editor of your local newspaper. Support political candidates who are working to protect our environment for future generations, and vote out narrow-minded politicians who don't get the big picture.

TEN TIPS WHEN INTRODUCING A FRIEND TO SURFING

So you told your buddy who surfs that you'd like to learn to surf and he agreed to teach you. Fantastic! But before you hit the waves, share this checklist with your friend and make him sign it. More than one friendship has been strained when the surfing friend totally sand-bagged his buddy and put him in over his head. (Sorry Erik!)

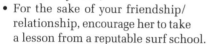

- For the sake of your friendship/ relationship, encourage her to take a lesson from a reputable surf school.
- Start them out with proper equipment. Put your friend on a big, fat soft surf-board. Leave your old 5'6" thruster in your closet.
- Lend your buddy a decent wetsuit if the water is cold enough to require one. Don't keep your 4/3 for yourself and give him your ratty old spring suit or farmer john.
- Take her out to an uncrowded beginner break, not your local gladiator pit.
- Orient him to the break by telling him where he should be, where the chan- nel is, and what to do if he can't make it outside.
- Show her how to turn turtle.
- Make sure he knows basic surf etiquette and won't kill anyone (or, worse, drop in on anyone).
- Make sure she is balanced properly on the board when paddling and that her legs are together. Otherwise she will not be able to paddle efficiently and may never catch a wave.
- Tell him to protect his head when he wipes out, and to stay underwater for a few seconds before coming up.

- Resist the urge to show off gratuitously. Showering her with spray while you cut back inches from her face doesn't help her learn or gain confidence.
- Keep an eye on him and check in on him from time to time.

I,_____, agree to abide by these rules and promise not to sandbag my friend.

Index